Islamic Theology

Ex dono Dr. Clive Holes
socii 1999.

Islamic Theology

Traditionalism and Rationalism

Binyamin Abrahamov

Edinburgh University Press

To Michael Schwarz

Edinburgh University Press
22 George Square, Edinburgh

Typeset in Baskerville
by Koinonia, Bury, and
printed and bound in Great Britain
by The University Press, Cambridge

A CIP record for this book is available
from the British Library

ISBN 0 7486 1102 9 (paperback)

CONTENTS

INTRODUCTION

It is a common human phenomenon that tradition and reason may oppose each other, mainly because tradition causes continuity, and hence stability, while reason causes change, and hence instability. Tradition is usually traced back to a great authority such as the teachings of great ancestors, while reason is based on personal efforts and does not submit to external authority. In the domain of religion, the debate between tradition and reason is sharper than in other domains, for tradition has the authority of divine revelation. However, tradition and reason may be harmonised and may complete each other. The Greek philosophers had set forth rational proofs for the existence of God[1] and arguments against popular religion,[2] and the history of the great monotheistic religions, Judaism, Christianity and Islam, attests to the dispute between reason and tradition and to the attempts to make them compatible. Muslim philosophers have dealt extensively with the relationship between philosophy and revelation, generally coming to the conclusion, whose source is neo-Platonic, that the notions contained in the Scriptures are symbols of the philosophic truth.[3] The strife between Muslim philosophers and traditional theologians gave birth to works dealing with a variety of issues, for example al-Ghazālī's (d. 505/1111) *Tahāfut al-falāsifa* (*The Incoherence of the Philosophers*)[4] and to books and chapters which treat specific issues such as the eternity of the world, God's ignorance of the particulars, the Resurrection and logic.[5] The relatively narrow scope of this debate seems to be due to the fact that philosophy has not penetrated into wide circles of Muslims, who, as a result, have not felt threatened by the philosophers' teachings. The philosophers for their part felt sometimes that there was no common ground to debate with the theologians. The Christian philosopher Yaḥyā ibn ʿAdī (d. 363/974) accused the Mutakallimūn of not fully understanding Aristotle's *Kitāb al-jadal* (*Topica*).[6]

The principal theological struggle in Islam, for which we have relatively numerous pieces of evidence, has taken place between traditionalist theologians and rationalist ones. The latter are represented by the Mutakallimūn, the speculative theologians, whether Muʿtazilites, Ashʿarites, Māturīdites or other groups. We should immediately note that the boundaries between these two groups of theologians, the traditionalists and the rationalists, are not always definitely marked. This will be elucidated later. Whereas in the dispute between philosophy and tradition, the traditionalists themselves are almost absent and it is carried out between theologians and philosophers, in the dispute between speculative theology and tradition, the traditionalists participated fully and brought forward arguments which refute the rationalists' notions. Concerning the issue of reason versus tradition, modern scholars seem to have devoted more attention to the thought of the philosophers, the Mutakallimūn and the sectarians than to the thought of the scholars who belong to the central trend of Islam, namely, the theologians of 'the people of the Sunna and the Consensus' (*ahl al-sunna wa'l-jamāʿa*), those who usually have not used Kalām speculation in their works, or have limited their use of speculative arguments to a minimum. A major part of the arguments of this trend demonstrates intellectual consistency and sophistication. The centrality of this struggle in Islamic thought, and the fact that modern scholars have paid little attention to it,[7] justify treating this subject again. Thus, the present work aims at examining the foundations of both traditionalism and rationalism in classical Islamic thought, the criticism levelled by each system of thought against the other and the attempts which have been carried out to reconcile reason and tradition. It is not a historical study, in the sense of retracing the development of arguments and systems of thought, although sometimes we shall show such developments (see below, Chapter 2, n. 42), partly because the foundations of traditionalism have not changed to a great extent over the ages;[8] rather, it identifies trends and directions. The materials studied are from the third/ninth century until the tenth/sixteenth century.[9] I have not tried to be exhaustive – it is impossible in such a work – but I have tried to give examples for each trend or notion, assuming that such trends and notions which will be discussed below occur also in materials which have not been dealt with here.

One of these issues is the conclusion arrived at in the present study that pure or extreme traditionalism does not belong exclusively to the Ḥanbalites, but also to the Shāfiʿite, the Mālikite and

Ḥanafite scholars. Another issue is the question of the attitude towards a sinner or an innovator in religion. As is well known, the orthodox (*ahl al-sunna*) neither considered the sinner and the innovator an unbeliever nor prevented prayer behind him. This attitude is confirmed by Ibn Taymiyya's statement, which constitutes the title of a chapter, to the effect that the traditionalists neither declare Muslims to be unbelievers on account of a sin or an innovation, nor prevent prayer behind them.[10] However, as we shall see, some Shāfiʿite scholars adopted a severe attitude towards sinners and innovators, including considering them unbelievers and the prohibition of praying behind them. Thus the Ḥanbalites were not always those who adopted extreme stands. The fact that Muslim scholars have not always been committed to the teachings of their schools as expressed by some eminent members of those schools has been already stated by G. Makdisi.[11]

I would like now to clarify the basic terms which are used in the present work. The word 'tradition' means literally handing over, but it also includes the object of handing over,[12] which, in our case, is practices or beliefs. The words or deeds of Muḥammad and his earlier followers, the Companions (*al-ṣaḥāba*) and their Followers (*tābiʿūn*), were handed down to posterity in a kind of communication which is called *ḥadīth* (a tradition, literally a tale or a report). The *ḥadīth* tells the Muslims Muḥammad's norms and beliefs (*sunna*, pl. *sunan*) which they must carry out and in which they must believe.[13] The people who have dealt with the *ḥadīth*, that is, those who have transmitted, criticised and compiled traditions, are called in this work 'traditionists' (*ahl al-ḥadīth* or *muḥadiththūn*). This term should be differentiated from 'traditionalists', namely, those who have regarded religious knowledge as deriving from the Revelation (the Qur'ān), the Tradition (the Sunna) and the Consensus (*ijmāʿ*) and preferred these sources to reason in treating religious matters. The traditionalists are mostly named *ahl al-sunna wa'l-jamāʿa* (The people of the Tradition and the Consensus).[14] It seems to me that the most common expression omits the Qur'ān, for it was evident that all Muslim sects believed in the Qur'ān, but some groups did not adhere to the Sunna.[15] Consequently, this designation has polemic overtones.

In the present study, the term 'rationalism', with which I am not completely satisfied, means the tendency to consider reason the principal device or one of the principal devices to reach the truth in religion, and the preference of reason to revelation and tradition in dealing with some theological matters, mainly when a conflict arises between them. In Islamic thought, those who held that reason is man's *sole* authority in attaining the truth were regarded as unbelievers, and as such they fall outside the scope of this study.[16] When we speak of rationalists in our context, we mean those who attacked the traditionalists and their doctrines on the basis of reason, claiming that much, but not all, of religious knowledge can be known through reason. The term 'rationalism' must be distinguished from 'rationality' which means treating any issue by using reason, but without giving reason priority. Rationality turns to rationalism when reason is prior to revelation. If a thinker proves God's existence and unity through rational proofs without having recourse to the Qur'ān and the Sunna as primary sources, he becomes a rationalist *in these subject matters.* A traditionalist may be rational in dealing with a theological issue – this phenomenon will also be discussed – but he may not ascribe to reason any advantage over the Qur'ān or the Sunna. His point of departure is the sacred texts.[17] Figures like Ibn Ḥanbal and Ibn Taymiyya have used reason in treating theological matters; Ibn Taymiyya claimed that the notion of using reason occurs in the Qur'ān, and hence there is no contradiction between revelation and reason.[18] Within Islam there is no pure rationalism, in the sense that all religious issues derive from reason. There are different degrees of rationalism; the most rationalist group is the Muʿtazila who used reason as a source of knowledge in many theological issues, whereas the Ashʿarites are less rationalist than the Muʿtazilites. But there is pure traditionalism. Traditionalists who have not used reason in deriving the principles of religion can be called pure traditionalists. Those among the traditionalists who have used reason in proving some of the principles of religion were sometimes called *mutakallimū ahl al-ḥadīth* (the speculative theologians of the people of Tradition).[19] Al-Ashʿarī represents a Mutakallim of *ahl al-ḥadīth*; when he proves the existence of God on the basis of the doctrine of atoms and accidents,[20] he is a rationalist, for he does not rely on the Qur'ān to prove this idea. The Qur'ān serves him only as corroboration. The same term applies to any theologian who has recourse to reason instead of tradition in proving a theological notion. Thus the term 'rationalist' applies to a Muslim theologian only in a certain or in some issues; it cannot be used without reservations.[21] It seems to me that *ahl al-ḥadīth* represents the highest degree of traditionalism, whereas other traditionalists allowed a certain measure of reason in dealing with theological problems. Ibn Taymiyya represents the rational trend of traditionalism. In spite of his adherence to the Qur'ān, the Sunna and the Consensus of the Salaf, he does not regard the Qur'ān as only a report (*khabar*) but as a device which teaches man rational arguments. However, he does not become a rationalist, because even when he uses rational proofs, he ascribes them to the Qur'ān. Thus Ibn Taymiyya remains in the framework of rationality and not of rationalism. Sometimes, for the same theological issue, there are two solutions, one traditional and the other rational. When speaking of Paradise, al-Baghdādī states that there is a rational possibility of the passing away of Paradise, but according to the Tradition Paradise will exist forever.[22] It is worth noting that a diversity of opinions concerning the source of theological doctrine has existed even among the Mu'tazilites, the most rationalist group of the Mutakallimūn. 'The command or the urge to do what is approved and the prohibition against doing what is reprehensible' (*al-amr bi'l-ma'rūf wa'l-nahy 'an al-munkar*), which is one of the five principles of the Mu'tazila,[23] is learned by some Mu'tazilites both from reason and revelation and by others from revelation only.[24]

This study focuses on the foundations of both traditionalism and rationalism, the arguments which the two tendencies used against each other and the compromise made by some thinkers between them. In the following, we shall discuss the foundations of traditionalism (Chapter 1), the place of reason in traditionalism (Chapter 2), Traditionalism against rationalism (Chapter 3), including the traditionalists' criticism of the use of rational methods and the attitude towards the Kalām and the Mutakallimūn, the foundations of rationalism (Chapter 4), the rationalists' criticism of traditionalism (Chapter 5) and the compromise between traditionalism and rationalism (Chapter 6). The appendices include a creed and texts which clarify some of the problems discussed.

1

THE FOUNDATIONS OF TRADITIONALISM

We have learned the foundations of traditionalism from the traditionalists' creeds, counsels to their followers and statements. The hierarchy of these foundations is established by us according to the texts, although they do not all make mention of all these foundations.

The first foundation of traditionalism in medieval Islam is the *strict* adherence to the teachings of the Qur'ān, the Sunna of the Prophet and the Consensus (*ijmā'*) mainly of the first generations of scholars.[1] This foundation is characteristic not only of the Ḥanbalites, who have been described in the scholarly literature as the main proponents of traditionalism, but also of members of other schools of law, for example the Shāfi'ites. The Shāfi'ite theologian al-Taymī (d. 535/1140) emphasises the role of the Qur'ān and the Sunna:

> The people of truth make the Qur'ān and the Sunna their model (*imām*) and they search for religion through both of them. What they have attained through their intellect and mind, they subject to the examination of the Book and the Sunna. If they find it compatible with both of them, they accept it, and they thank God for showing them this and for His guidance. If they find it opposing the Qur'ān and the Sunna, they leave what they have attained and turn to both of them and blame themselves (for finding such a notion). That is because the Book and the Sunna guide the people only to the truth, while man's opinion may be true or false.[2]

Thus the Book and the Sunna serve not only as the source of truth but also as the criterion for examining what man obtains through his intellect. One should note that some of the ideas of traditionalism were developed by Shāfi'ite theologians and appeared later in Ḥanbalite works.[3]

Let us examine an example of adherence to the Qur'ān, the Sunna and the Consensus in dealing with a specific theological issue. In the Shāfi'ite scholar al-Lālakā'ī (d. 418/1027), the discussion of predestination begins with interpretation of Qur'ān verses through the device of *al-tafsīr bi'l-ma'thūr* (interpretation through putting forth traditions). Qur'ān 37.96 'God has created you and your action' (*allah khalaqakum wa-mā ta'malūna*) is interpreted, according to a tradition traced back to Ḥudhayfa ibn al-Yamān (d. 36/656), to mean that God creates people and their actions.[4] Likewise, the verse 'We have created everything through a decree' (Qur'ān 54.49) is interpreted by 'Abdallāh ibn 'Abbās (d. 68/687) to mean that God has created all people through a decree and also that He has created good and evil.[5] In the same manner, al-Lālakā'ī interprets dozens of verses and then cites traditions independent of the Qur'ān verses.[6] The third phase in al-Lālakā'ī's discussion of God's predetermination sets forth the consensus of Muhammad's Companions and their Followers through citations of their statements which advocate God's predetermination.[7] He neither uses speculative reasons nor compares verses or traditions in order to draw theological conclusions. Thus al-Lālakā'ī follows the dictum adopted by some traditionalists, to the effect that there is no analogy in the Sunna (*laysa fī'l-sunna qiyās*). By analogy, they mean any speculative argument which may answer the theological questions of how and why.[8] The prohibition against dealing with God's essence (*la tafakkarū fī dhāt allāh*)[9] through using rational proofs is a part of this rule. The Qur'ān and the Sunna contain what man should know and believe,[10] and therefore any discussion involving external devices such as rational arguments is rejected. It is in this framework that one should place the prohibition stated in several traditions of dealing with the problem of God's predetermination.[11] Thus extreme (or pure) traditionalists consider speculative reasoning concerning theological issues as something to be avoided. They sometimes go so far in their adherence to the Qur'ān and the Sunna as to say that whoever refutes one verse of the Qur'ān refutes the whole Qur'ān, and the same with regard to the Sunna.[12]

When these three elements of traditionalism, the Qur'ān, the Sunna and the Consensus, are joined together, they lead to certain and true perceptions which no interpretation can oppose. Concerning the issue of man's seeing God in the world to come, al-Dārimī (d. 280/893) says: 'If the Qurā'n, the Messenger's saying and the Consensus of the community join, there is no other interpretation'.[13]

Here it is appropriate to treat the authoritativeness of the three principles of traditionalism, for the discussion of this subject is relevant to the adherence to them. Basing the authoritativeness of these three principles justifies and strengthens their acceptance, and rejects the rationalists' claim to use reason as proof of theological tenets. However, there is a difference between the Qur'ān on the one hand and the Sunna and the Consensus on the other. While the authoritativeness of the Qur'ān derives from its being divine and eternal speech[14] – although in Arabic literature there have been a few attempts to criticise its contents and style[15] – the proofs of the authoritativeness of the Sunna and the Consensus were discussed at length by Muslim scholars. One of the ways taken to establish the authoritativeness of the Sunna, certainly – as the context proves – with the aim of refuting those who have attacked the Tradition (see below, pp. 41ff.), namely the rationalists, was to equal it to the Qur'ān. In a tradition quoted by al-Lālakā'ī, Jibrīl is said to have sent down (*kāna yunzilu*) the Sunna on Muḥammad and to have taught him its contents just as he did with regard to the Qur'ān.[16] In *Sharḥ al-Sunna,* a work by the Shāfi'ite scholar al-Ḥusayn ibn Mas'ūd al-Baghawī (d. 516/1122), Muḥammad is quoted as saying that he was given the Book with what resembles it. According to al-Baghawī, Muḥammad received the unrecited texts, the Sunan, just as he received the recited text, the Qur'ān. As a corroboration, he cites Qur'ān 3.164 'Truly God was gracious to the believers when He raised up among them a Messenger from themselves, to recite to them His signs and to purify them, and to teach them the Book and the Wisdom, though before they were in manifest error' (tr. Arberry). The Book is the Qur'ān and the Wisdom (*ḥikma*) is the Sunna.[17] The adherence to the Qur'ān and the Sunna is a title which occurs in the Ḥadīth literature. Here the Ḥadīth is legitimised through the Ḥadīth itself.[18]

Four centuries after al-Baghawī, the famous Shāfi'ite scholar Jalāl al-Dīn al-Suyūṭī (d. 911/1505) tried to vindicate the use of the Sunna as a tool equal to the Qur'ān in religious matters. His work entitled *Miftāḥ al-janna fī'l-i'tiṣām bi'l-sunna* (The Key to Paradise is the Adherence to the Sunna) begins with a statement made by a Shī'ite (*rāfiḍī*) to the effect that traditions should not be employed as arguments and that only in the Qur'ān should one find one's arguments. Paradoxically, in support of his contention, this Shī'ite brings as evidence a tradition according to which the Prophet says that 'You should subject any tradition coming from me to the judgement of the Qur'ān, then, if you find its root in the Qur'ān you should accept it, otherwise, you should reject it'.[19] Thus the Qur'ān judges the Sunna, which has no independent status, and the Qur'ān contains the criteria of what man must know. However, according to al-Suyūṭī, whoever denies that a prophetic tradition may be used as an argument is an unbeliever.[20] Basing himself on great authorities such as al-Shāfi'ī (d. 205/820) and Abū Bakr Aḥmad ibn al-Ḥusayn al-Bayhaqī (d. 458/1065), he states that the Qur'ān (4.171, 24.62 and 3.164 cited above) connects the belief in Muḥammad with the belief in God and that God orders the Muslims to follow His revelation as well as the Prophet's traditions (*faraḍa Allāh 'alā al-nās ittibā' waḥyihi wa-sunan rasūlihi*).[21] The Sunna is compared to the Qur'ān in traditions which state that if the believers adhere to the Qur'ān and the Sunna they will never err.[22] The equalisation of the Sunna to the Qur'ān is expressed also from three other points of view: (1) the Sunna was sent down like the Qur'ān;[23] (2) the Sunna should be studied as the Qur'ān is studied;[24] (3) the sanctity (or inviolability, *ḥurma*) of the Messenger's traditions is like that of the Qur'ān.[25] This last notion is also expressed in a slightly different manner in another tradition cited by the Mālikite scholar Abū 'Umar Yūsuf ibn 'Abd al-Barr (d. 463/1070). It reads: 'What God's Messenger prohibited (*mā ḥarrama rasūl allāh*) is like what God prohibited (*mithl mā ḥarrama allāh*)'.[26] Again, in the context of refuting the rationalists, there appears the view that the Sunna contains what the believer should know. Al-Suyūṭī, basing himself on Abū Bakr al-Khaṭīb al-Baghdādī's (d. 463/1070) *Sharaf aṣḥāb al-ḥadīth,* says that whoever is content with the Tradition does not need anything else, for it contains the principles of religion, such as God's unity, His attributes, the prophets' stories, history, the biography of the Prophet, Qur'ān interpretation, laws and so on.[27]

In sum, the authoritativeness of the Sunna is proved not only because it is the summa of the Prophet's sayings and actions which were transmitted through chains of reliable Muslims, but also through the idea that the Sunna is equal to the Qur'ān in rank and, hence, should be regarded as such. Thus the Qur'ān is not the sole Islamic revelation.

The authoritativeness of the Consensus (*ḥujjiyyat al-ijmā'*) has been thoroughly discussed by Hourani.[28] *Ijmā'* is sometimes based on the Qur'ān, for example, Qur'ān 4.115, from which one can learn that man must follow the 'way of the believers' which amounts to consensus.[29] Sometimes it is based on prophetic traditions such as 'what the believers regard as good is good in God's eyes and what they regard as evil is evil in God's eyes'[30] or 'my community does not agree on an error',[31] and the trustworthiness of the tradition itself is based on *tawātur.*[32] The attitude towards reason as a means to prove the authoritativeness of the Consensus is not definite. Although most of the *uṣulis* (those who treat the subject of the principles of law – *uṣul al-fiqh*) did not consider reason a source for proving the authoritativeness of consensus, some of them did attempt to do so.[33] According to Hourani, generally in the discussions of the basis of *ijmāʿ* the kind of group which constitutes the *ijmāʿ* is not specified.[34] I have the impression, however, that many traditionalists regard the consensus of the first generations of Muslim community, especially the Companions of the Prophet and their Followers, as the best consensus. Contrary to Hourani,[35] not only the Ḥanbalites regard the *ijmāʿ* of the ancient scholars as obligatory, but, as we shall see, so do scholars of other schools of thought.[36]

In this context, it is worth noting the meaning of the word *jamāʿa* (literally 'group'), which occurs in the term *ahl al-sunna wa'l-jamāʿa.* According to al-Shāṭibī in his *al-Iʿtiṣām*[37] as quoted by al-Lālakā'ī,[38] Muslim scholars have five definitions of *jamāʿa*: (1) the majority of the Muslims; (2) the leading scholars of the Muslim community; (3) Muḥammad's Companions; (4) all Muslims when they agree on a certain matter; (5) all Muslims when they agree on a certain leader. Generally, the extreme traditionalists adopt the second or the third definition or both of them,[39] while the moderate wing of traditionalism speaks of the consensus of the community. In al-Lālakā'ī, many traditions enjoin Muslims to adhere to the community (*al-jamāʿa*). Among them is a tradition traced back to ʿUmar which tells that the best people are the *Ṣaḥāba*; those who came after them are inferior and so forth until lies will diffuse. In this case, one should have recourse to the community, since the Devil exists with the individual. The *jamāʿa,* then, is presented as a device which prevents people from believing in lies.[40] Although the best consensus remains that of the *Ṣaḥāba,* that of the community is not rejected.

The need to adhere to the public (*jamāʿa*) is stated by the Ḥanbalite scholar Ibn al-Jawzī (d. 597/1200) by means of a tradition traced back to ʿUmar ibn al-Khaṭṭāb, which reads: 'Whoever wants the pleasure of Paradise must join the community (*al-jamāʿa*), for the Devil exists with the individual and he is remotest from the two'.[41] According to other traditions, God protects the community, and whoever leaves the community may be liable to the Devil's attack, like a sheep which may be liable to the wolf's attack when it leaves the flock. God unites the people for the purpose of their keeping the right way.[42] *Jamāʿa* is the opposite of *iftirāq* (division), and division causes perdition. The adherence to the community, meaning the consensus, serves as a guarantee to the preservation of the Muslims. Uniformity protects any group of people from being led astray. Hence, dispute (*jadal*) should be rejected.[43] As we shall immediately see, the holding of different opinions, which endangers the community, also appears in polemical context when dealing with the principle of homogeneity.

The second foundation of traditionalism is the idea that the principles of religion, which derive from the above-mentioned roots, namely, the Qur'ān, the Sunna and the Consensus, are homogeneous. Hence, any disagreement concerning these principles is reprehensible. Referring to Qur'ān 3.105, 'Be not as those who scattered (*tafarraqū*) and fell into variance (*ikhtalafū*) after the clear signs (*bayyināt*) came to them' (tr. Arberry), the Shāfiʿite scholar al-Bayhaqī (d. 458/1065) states that the Qur'ān, the Sunna and the Consensus of Muḥammad's Companions have affirmed God's attributes (*ṣifāt*),[44] the believers' seeing of God in the World to Come (*ru'yat allāh*)[45] and the Intercession (*shafāʿa*).[46] Whoever denies these principles and contradicts them does so after the coming of the clear signs, meaning the Qur'ān, the Sunna and the Consensus. Al-Bayhaqī adds that the Prophet's Companions have agreed on the principles of religion, and as for the branches (*furū*, the laws), which stem from these principles, and matters for which there is no text either in the Qur'ān or in the Sunna, they have agreed on some of them and disagreed on others.[47] The Law-giver (*ṣāḥib al-shar*) has allowed his Companions this kind of disagreement which originates from the system of deriving conclusions (*istinbāṭ*) and the system of formulating independent judgements (*ijtihād*).[48]

Apart from introducing traditions which defame dispute (*jadal*) in theological issues, such as 'They [meaning the ancient scholars] hated diversity in religion (*al-dīn*)' or 'Beware of debates in religion',[49] the traditionalists tried to prove the principle of homogeneity by referring to real experiences of scholars. The famous traditionist Muḥammad ibn Ismāʿīl al-Bukhārī (d. 257/870) says that over forty-six years he has met more than 1,000 scholars from different districts – some of the most prominent of them are indicated – all of whom were agreed upon the tenets of Islam.[50] A similar notion appears in a creed related by two scholars of Rayy, Abū Zurʿa ʿUbayd

Allāh ibn ʿAbd al-Karīm (d. 264/878) and Abū Ḥātim Muḥammad ibn Idrīs ibn al-Mundhir (d. 277/890), who were critics of Ḥadīth.[51] Both of them stated that the scholars from all the cities in Ḥijāz, al-ʿIrāq, al-Shām and al-Yaman had agreed on the same articles of faith.[52] According to Ibn Qutayba, the traditionists (*ahl al-ḥadīth*) are characterised by agreement and homogeneity.[53] It seems that the underlying assumption of the traditionalists, who sought homogeneity, was the idea that adhering to the same sources, the Qur'ān, the Sunna and the Consensus, would bring about identical results.[54] Also the tendency to stress the prophetic tradition was the result of the aspiration to homogeneity.[55]

A part of the notion of homogeneity is the polemical statement that while the Mutakallimūn move from one notion to another, the traditionalists are stable and do not change their minds even if they are subjected to severe trials. Stability in one's opinions is a sign of certain belief and truth. In Ibn Taymiyya, agreement in views, absence of divergencies and, hence, stability serve as criteria for measuring one's proximity to truth. Thus, for example, the differences in the philosophers' notions testify to their remoteness from truth.[56] Uniformity, which is the outcome of following the Qur'ān and the Sunna, causes stability, and also serves the aim of preserving the community from destruction. Nations have perished because of heresies.[57]

As a result of the above-mentioned notion, one should not accept without reservation Goldziher's statement that 'indeed, the conception of diversity as a divine favour was not limited to the *ikhtilāf al-fuqahā* (dissent among legal experts), but was extended even to doctrinal difference' ('Catholic Tendencies and Particularism in Islam', p. 130). Goldziher rightly points out that orthodox Islam never produced formal institutions for the establishing of dogmas (ibid.), but ignores the fact that uniformity in matters of theology may be achieved, as indeed happened, through informal dynamism motivated by the strict adherence to the Qur'ān, the Sunna and the Consensus.

A logical consequence of following the Sunna of the Prophet is the adherence to those who are responsible for the collection and transmission of traditions, which is the third foundation of traditionalism. In the first rank stand Muḥammad's Companions (*Ṣaḥāba*)[58] and their Followers (*Tābiʿūn*). In the second rank stand *ahl al-ḥadīth* or *aṣḥāb al-ḥadīth*, meaning the people who deal with traditions, or, as we have stated, the traditionists. The *Ṣaḥāba* are the best, the purest and the most just people whom God has chosen. This is proved through Qur'ān verses and traditions.[59] Praises of Muḥammad's Companions and apologia for them *in extensive form* occur not only in Ḥanbalite literature, but also in writings of scholars who affiliated with other schools of law.[60] Abū Bakr ibn al-Arabī al-Muʿāfirī (d. 543/1148), an eminent scholar of the Mālikite school, wrote a book entitled *al-ʿAwāṣim min al-qawāṣim, fī taḥqīq mawāqif al-ṣaḥāba baʿda wafāt al-nabī ṣallā allāh ʿalayhi wa-sallama* ('The Defence against Attack, on the Verification of the Companions' Stands after Muḥammad's Death'). A general survey of the traditions dealing with the *Ṣaḥāba* in al-Lālakā'ī's *sharḥ uṣūl* shows the importance ascribed to the adherence to them. These traditions occupy the seventh and eighth parts of al-Lālakā'ī's work. It is stated there that the love for the *Ṣaḥāba* stems from the Sunna, and people are urged to love them. People are forbidden to abuse the *Ṣaḥāba*, and God will curse and punish severely whoever abuses them. Many traditions are devoted to the praises of the first four caliphs and other eminent *Ṣaḥābī*s such as Talḥa, al-Zubayr and Abū ʿUbayda. That the idealisation of the pious ancestors is an important part of traditionalism is also demonstrated through the creeds of all the schools of Law. The creed of the Mālikite jurist Ibn Abī Zayd al-Qayrawānī (d. 386/996) states:

> The best of generations is the generation who saw the Messenger of God and believed in him. Next are those who followed them, and next are those who followed these. The most excellent of the Companions (of Muḥammad) are the rightly and truly guided caliphs, Abū Bakr, then ʿUmar, then ʿUthmān, then ʿAlī. Let not any of the Companions of the Messenger be mentioned except most honourably and without reference to what was disputed among them. They, above other people, deserve to have the best construction put upon (their conduct) and to have the best views attributed to them.[61]

However, in al-Lālakā'ī's view the term *ahl al-ḥadīth* includes not only those who transmit traditions but also those who transmit and recite the Qur'ān, because one of the Qur'ān's names is *ḥadīth* (Qur'ān 39.23 'God has sent down the fairest discourse', *aḥsan al-ḥadīth* ...), and because people learn the Qur'ān from them.[62] The traditionists are highly praised, for they are the bearers of God's knowledge and religion and are the mediators between God and His community. Their influence on the community is great in their life, because of their pietistic conduct, and after their death they are also venerated through the visiting of their tombs.[63] Ibn Taymiyya gives Ibn Ḥanbal's funeral, in which thousands of people participated, as an example of adoration for those who follow the Sunna. Likewise, al-Shāfiʿī and other scholars were glorified by many people, for they adhered to the Sunna.[64] Some scholars, like Ibn Ḥazm, were honoured only when they adhered to the Sunna, but criticised whenever they deviated from it.[65]

Until now we have dealt with the positive elements of traditionalism, namely, the adherence to the Qur'ān, the Sunna and the Consensus, homogeneity of ideas and the following of the traditionists. However, traditionalism also has negative foundations which are no less extensively dealt with in the religious literature. Contrary to adherence to the Qur'ān, the Sunna and the Consensus stands the opposition to any innovation (*bidʿa*) which is regarded as going astray (*ḍalāla*).[66] Just as the source of the truth is adherence to unchanged and definite principles, so the source of deviation and innovation is adherence to different, changeable principles.[67] And contrary to the following of the traditionists, there is a clear opposition to the innovators which takes various forms.

One of these forms is the prohibition against disputing with (*munāẓara*) the innovators (*ahl al-bidaʿ*), speaking with them and listening to their innovative views.[68] The estimation of the innovators' religious stand is obviously expressed in the notion that they are regarded as those who cannot repent of their innovation, whereas sinners can repent of their sins.[69] This means that innovation is even graver than polytheism, for a polytheist may change his status and become a Muslim, whereas an innovator remains in his status. According to the Ḥanbalite scholar Ibn al-Jawzī (d. 597/1200), not only the innovators but also those who sit with them are dangerous to Islam.[70] The reason for this is the following tradition: 'Whoever helps (in another version "honours") an innovator helps to destroy Islam'.[71] The innovator is so abominable a person that even if he walked on water (a reference to Jesus' miracle) or on air, he would not be accepted by the pious people. A certain Bishr ibn al-Ḥārith is reported to have said: 'While I was walking in the market I heard about the death of al-Marīsī.[72] If the market had been a place of prostration, I would have prostrated myself, thanking God and praising Him for killing him.'[73]

As we have seen, a part of the rejection of any innovation is the prohibition against dealing with metaphysical issues,[74] such as God's attributes and essence, or predetermination. One of the traditions which expresses this prohibition is: 'Think of (*tafakkarū*) God's creation and not of Him' (in another version 'His essence' (*dhāt*).[75] This prohibition is one of the foundations of the *bi-lā kayfa* doctrine with which I have dealt in my 'The *bi-lā kayfa* Doctrine and Its Foundations in Islamic Theology'. Al-Lālakā'ī devotes a chapter (vol. 2, pp. 627ff.) to the prohibition against treating the problem of predestination (*qadar*). He quotes the renowned tradition which reads: 'Do not speak of anything relating to *qadar*, for it is God's secret, so do not disclose God's secret'.[76] One is forbidden to deal with predestination because it leads to heresy (*zandaqa*).[77] The ban on associating with the people of *qadar*[78] arises logically out of the ban on treating the *qadar* problem.[79] The Qadarites are regarded as God's adversaries, as the Zoroastrians of this community (*majūs hādhihi al-umma*),[80] and as those who will bring destruction to their community. The Children of Israel are brought forward as an example of a community which caused itself destruction on account of their controversy over this question.[81] The Qadarites are also considered unbelievers and, hence, their punishment is death.[82] The traditionalists' attitude towards the Qadarites is best exemplified by the prohibitions against praying behind them, marrying them, eating animals slaughtered by them, and accepting their testimonies.[83] They also accuse those who adhere to heretical views[84] of unbelief.

Contrary to the explicit prohibition against disputing with the innovators, one can find a trend which allows such a dispute and even recommends how it should be carried out. According to a tradition traced back to 'Umar ibn al-Khaṭṭāb and quoted by several authorities,[85] there will come a time in which people will dispute *ahl al-sunna wa'l-jamā'a* through using the ambiguous verses of the Qur'ān (*shubuhāt al-qur'ān*). The tradition advises the scholars to employ traditions in this dispute, for those who are experts in traditions know the Qur'ān best.[86] We also learn here the value of traditions in disputes concerning the Qur'ān. Al-Suyūṭī, stating that the Qur'ān, contrary to the Sunna, has many aspects (*dhū wujūh*),[87] justifies the use of traditions in polemics on the Qur'ān. It is related that 'Alī ibn Abī Ṭālib sent Ibn 'Abbās to dispute with the Khārijites; he was ordered to dispute on the basis of traditions, not the Qur'ān, because the Qur'ān has many aspects, otherwise the dispute would take the shape of 'we say' and 'they say' (*naqūlu wa-yaqūlūna*), in other words, a dispute without victory for either side. Ibn 'Abbās did as he was ordered and the Khārijites were unable to argue against him.[88] It is also characteristic of the traditionalists to resort to arguments which, according to them, are definitive by virtue of their nature and, hence, cannot be refuted.

A further elaboration of the attitude of the traditionalists towards the rationalists will be set forth in Chapter 3, which deals specifically with the traditionalists' attitude towards the Kalām and the Mutakallimūn. The present issue belongs to this chapter and the next.

2

THE PLACE OF REASON IN TRADITIONALISM

Both the traditionalists and the rationalists use reason, but there is generally a clear difference between the two parties with respect to the status of reason within their systems. This difference is perspicuously stated by al-Taymī. According to him,[1] the innovators base their doctrines on reason (*ʿaql*), while stating that traditions are subject to reason. The traditionalists, on the other hand, say that the basis of religion is following the traditions, and reason comes after traditions. They argue that if religion were based on reason, people would not need revelation and prophets,[2] the orders and the prohibitions would be cancelled and people would follow their wills. Moreover, it would be possible for the believers not to accept anything unless it appears reasonable to them. In al-Taymī's view, there are many issues in religion, such as God's attributes, Paradise and Hell, the Punishment in the Tomb (*ʿadhāb al-qabr*), the Balance (*al-mīzān*) and so on, whose true meanings believers cannot perceive through reason, notwithstanding that they are obliged to believe in and to accept them. If people understand anything of religion, they must thank God, for He causes their understanding.[3] The right method of dealing with religious issues, which cannot be understood through reason, is not to make a decision (*tawqīf*) concerning such issues, and to delegate their knowledge to God (*tafwīḍ*).[4]

A similar notion is put forth by al-Lālakā'ī. He states that the necessity (*wujūb*) of man's knowledge of God and His attributes derives from the *samʿ* (here the meaning is the Qur'ān and the Sunna, but sometimes the term includes also the Consensus) and not from reason. To prove his statement, the author cites some verses, for example Qur'ān 47.19 'Know therefore that there is no god but God'; 6.106 'Follow what has been revealed to you from your Lord; there is no god but He; and turn away from the idolators'; 21.25 'And We sent never a Messenger before you except that we revealed to him, saying: "There is no god but I; so serve Me"'. Other verses show that the necessity of one's knowledge of the messengers also derives from the sacred texts, for example Qur'ān 7.158 'Believe in God and His Messenger ...'; 17.15 'We never chastise, until We send forth a Messenger'.[5] Traditions are put forth to show that God sent Muḥammad.[6]

The traditionalists, however, do not altogether annul the function of reason in religion, but assign to it a secondary function, namely, to prove what has been revealed or transmitted, or to know how to perform the precepts.[7] The attitude towards the notion of *taqlīd* may show the difference between the traditionalist and the rationalist positions. *Taqlīd* means following blindly someone else's teaching without bringing proofs or criticising.[8] Al-Taymī defines *taqlīd* as accepting someone else's view without a proof (*qabūl qawl al-ghayr min ghayri ḥujja*).[9] In his view, there is a clear difference between adherence to a doctrine (*ittibāʿ*) accompanied by proofs, and *taqlīd*.[10] The Qur'ān and the Sunna order man to adhere to their teachings but not to follow them blindly. Muslims have traditional proofs (*dalā'il samʿiyya*) which attest to Muḥammad's prophecy and which were transmitted to them by transmitters (*ruwāt*). After accepting the authenticity of Muḥammad's prophecy, Muslims are obliged to believe in the contents of his prophecy which comprises God's unity, His attributes and so on. As far as it is put forth by the Qur'ān and the Sunna, reflection (*naẓar*) in order to attain more certainty and tranquillity of the soul is not rejected.[11] Al-Taymī opposes the Mutakallimūn's stand according to which the first obligation on man is reflection (*naẓar*) which brings about knowledge of the Creator (*awwal mā yajibu ʿalā al-insān al-naẓar al-mu'addī ilā maʿrifat al-bārī*).[12] The arguments which he uses against this stand are based on tradition and reason. He asks, for example, 'How can it be that man's first obligation was hidden from the *Ṣaḥāba* who were the first leaders of this community and the mediators between Muḥammad and the Muslims?" And traditions, which were transmitted through the process of *tawātur*,[13] relate that Muḥammad called the unbelievers to Islam, and called upon them to express the two testimonies of the profession of faith (*shahādatayn*) and not to speculate.[14]

The traditionalists demonstrate their notions not only through traditional proofs but also through various rational proofs. Even traditionalists who are not primarily identified as Mutakallimūn used to employ rational arguments, sometimes even Kalām arguments, to prove traditional dogmas. Combining traditional and rational proofs is characteristic of many traditionalists. This phenomenon may be explained mainly by their polemics with the rationalists which frequently forced the traditionalists to use rational arguments. To illustrate the use of rational proofs, let us bring some examples. It is very fitting to begin with Ibn Ḥanbal, who has become down the ages a symbol of traditionalism. Ibn Ḥanbal refutes the Jahmites,[15] who argue that God is everywhere.[16] After quoting Qur'ān verses to the effect that God sat Himself upon the Throne (*istawā ʿalā al-ʿarsh*, Qur'ān 7.54, 20.5), he states that there are places, such as man's body, which are not appropriate for God's greatness (*ʿiẓam*). Thus it is impossible for God to be there.[17] This is a simple rational argument which is based on the contradiction between the Jahmites' contention and one of God's most beautiful names, namely, God's being the greatest (*ʿaẓīm*).[18] This argument appears later in al-Ashʿarī and in the writings of his successors.[19]

However, Ibn Ḥanbal also uses arguments characteristic of the Kalām. One of these is the argument from disjunction (*qisma* or *taqsīm*).[20] Concerning the issue just discussed, he asks the Jahmite whether God was without anything before creation. The Jahmite answers in the affirmative. Then Ibn Ḥanbal raises the following question: 'When God created a thing, did He create it inside Himself or outside Himself?' The answer to this question can be divided into three parts, only one of which is right. If the Jahmite argues that God created the creation inside Himself, he will be considered an unbeliever, for he argues that Jinn (demons), people and Devil are inside God. If he argues that God created the material world outside Himself then entered into them, this also will be unbelief, for he argues that God entered into dirty places. Finally, if he argues that God created His creation outside Himself then did not enter into them, he will withdraw his contention. This last possibility is the view of *ahl al-sunna*.[21]

Al-Lālakā'ī uses a way of proving known as *istinbāṭ*, which means to produce a logical argument based on a Qur'ān verse.[22] As an example, let us take the issue of the uncreatedness of the Qur'ān advanced by *ahl al-sunna*. The foundation of the argument is Qur'ān 36.82 'His command, when He desires a thing, is to say to it "Be" (*kun*), and it is'. This verse shows us that God creates everything by saying to it *kun*. Now, if *kun*, which is God's speech considered by the Muʿtazilites to be created, is also created, then a created thing created another created thing which leads to an uninterrupted chain of creations, which is an absurdity.[23] It is to be noted that the framework of the argument is a tradition. Another *istinbāṭ* is based on Qur'ān 7.54 'Verily, His are the creation (*khalq*) and the command (*amr*)'. God differentiates between the two words *khalq* and *amr*. *Khalq* means the created things (*makhlūqāt*), whereas *amr* is the Qur'ān, that is, God's uncreated speech.[24]

Al-Lālakā'ī reports a conversation between a certain person and Abū al-Hudhayl al-ʿAllāf (d. 235/850), the head of the Muʿtazilite school of Baṣra. Abū al-Hudhayl was asked about the Qur'ān and answered that it was created. The conversation continues as follows: Q: Does a created thing die or will it live forever? A: It will die. Q: When will the Qur'ān die? A: When those who recite the Qur'ān die, the Qur'ān will die. Q: [Suppose] those who recite the Qur'ān died and the world passed away, and then God would say: 'Whose is the Kingdom today?' (Qur'ān 40.16). This is [God's speech, namely] the Qur'ān. Although people already died [the Qur'ān still speaks, which means that it is eternal]. Abū al-Hudhayl answered to this: 'I do not know', and he was perplexed.[25] Without paying attention to the authenticity of this story, which does not matter here, this passage shows that the traditionalists, in this case al-Lālakā'ī, tried to refute their opponents through using reason and systems of Kalām.

Sometimes the traditionalists employ the technical terms of their opponents to prove that the latter contradict their own thesis, or cannot act according to it. Abū Isḥāq al-Shirāzī, a Shāfiʿite scholar (d. 476/1083), tells us about a dispute between one of the people of unity (*ahl al-tawḥīd*) and a Muʿtazilite, who is called here a *qadarī*.[26] They were both near a tree. The *qadarī* took a leaf from the tree and said: 'Did [not] I make or create [this action]?' (He thus referred to the Muʿtazilite doctrine that man makes or creates his actions.[27]) The traditionalist answered: 'If you are right, then return the leaf to its first condition, for whoever is capable of doing something is also capable of doing its opposite (*man qadara ʿalā shay' qadara ʿalā ḍiddihi*').[28] This is one of the components of the Muʿtazilite doctrine of man's creation of his acts.[29]

As I have pointed out elsewhere,[30] simple rational arguments are adduced to refute the figurative interpretations of anthropomorphic verses or traditions. One of these traditions tells about God's descent to the lowest heaven at the end of every night. In this event, God states: 'Whoever calls Me, I will answer him, whoever asks something, I will give him, and whoever asks forgiveness, I will forgive him'.[31] According to the figurative interpretation, it is not God who descends every night, but His command and mercy, for God is everywhere and His position does not change. The traditionalist scornfully attacks this argument saying that it belongs to the kind of arguments used by women and children. However, he does not content himself with *ad hominem* argument. In his view, their argument does not hold water, for God's command and mercy descends to the earth every minute, thus there is no need to particularise a part of the night for this descent. Moreover, does God call people to ask forgiveness through His command and mercy? Or does He make His command and mercy speak in His name? An affirmative answer to the last question obliges the opponent to ask the command and the mercy forgiveness, which is an absurdity. The traditionalist regards the opponent's stand as rejection of the truth even if the latter knows it (*mukābara*).[32]

Another argument used by al-Dārimī against al-Marīsī can be named as the *a fortiori* argument. Al-Dārimī states that 'we do not allow independent reasoning (*ijtihād al-ra'y*) in many juristic issues which we see and hear, the more so concerning God's attributes which we do not see and on which we cannot conjecture'.[33]

According to al-Marīsī, one must not interpret the word 'finger' which occurs in the famous tradition 'the people's hearts are between two of God's fingers'[34] as God's power (*qudra*). From the point of view of the Arabic language, says al-Dārimī, this interpretation is untenable, because the identification of 'finger' with 'power' is not found in any of the Arabic dialects. Moreover, people always speak of God's *power* and not of His *powers*.[35]

Linguistic considerations are also put forth when dealing with the problem of God's attributes. The Muʿtazilites distinguish between two kinds of attributes: essential attributes (*ṣifāt al-dhāt*) and factual attributes (*ṣifāt al-fiʿl*).[36] God is entitled to factual attributes only when He acts, whereas essential attributes are regarded as always inhering in Him. Consequently, the attributes Creator, Benefactor, Provider, and so on refer to God only after He creates, gives support, provides and so on. Thus they are not eternal and inherent attributes of Him. Al-Taymī refutes the notion of factual attributes through putting forth linguistic examples taken from the ordinary use of language. We say a cutting knife, a satiating bread and quenching water, for we know that cutting, satiating and quenching will come into effect through these three objects, even if now these acts do not exist. In like manner, God is the Creator, the Benefactor, the Provider and so on before He created, gave support and provided, for these acts will come into effect in the future on behalf of God.[37] It is worth noting that the Shāfiʿite traditionalist scholar al-Bayhaqī (d. 458/1065) accepted the Kalām distinction between essential attributes and factual attributes, emphasising that God always deserves the factual ones but not from eternity.[38]

Very important to our inquiry is al-Taymī's distinction between intellect (*'aql*) and knowledge (*'ilm*). First, quoting an anonymous scholar, he states definitely that religion is not perceived by the intellect (*al-dīn lā yudraku bi'l-'aql*). Then he states what he means by the intellect. The intellect is divided into two parts: inborn intellect (*'aql gharīzī*) and acquired intellect (*'aql iktisābī*). By the inborn intellect, one can abstain from damage and bring benefits to oneself. The inborn intellect grows in the course of a man's life until he reaches the age of forty (Qur'ān 46.15) whereupon his intellect is perfect. This growth is called acquired intellect. However, after the age of forty the intellect decreases as man becomes old and feeble-minded. Contrary to the decrease of the intellect after the age of forty, man's knowledge increases every day. Al-Taymī seems to understand knowledge as the accumulation of information in the mind, a process which does not stop. It must be admitted that the difference between these two kinds of intellect is not so clear, because what he calls acquired intellect seems to grow due to experience, which continues throughout life. Al-Taymī does not attempt to explain this obscurity. However, since the intellect stops its growth and attains its perfection at forty, whereas man never stops attaining knowledge, the intellect is weaker than knowledge. Consequently, owing to its weakness, religious issues cannot be perceived by the intellect, but, owing to the strength and multiplicity of knowledge, they can be perceived by knowledge.[39]

The judgement of the intellect, says al-Taymī, is different from the judgement of knowledge. Knowledge regards issues in religion as appropriate, whereas the intellect regards the same issues as inappropriate. For instance, sexual intercourse is rejected by the intellect, whereas knowledge and religious law deem it right. Furthermore, if the intellect had perceived religion, the rational persons (*'uqalā'*) among the unbelievers, especially the Qurayshites who were renowned for their intellectual ability, would not have insisted on unbelief. The chapter ends with the notion that knowledge is stronger than the intellect, because God is described as knowing (*'ālim*) and not as having intellect (*'āqil*).[40]

The Qur'ān is sometimes described as containing the rational proofs which the believer needs. For example, concerning the

Resurrection, the Qur'ān states that if God was able to create the world and man, it will be easier for Him to revive the dead (Qur'ān 17.50). Likewise, the Resurrection is compared to God's causing the earth to give birth to plants. Whoever can revive the earth can revive the dead (Qur'ān 35.9). And the existence of one Creator is proved through the argument that many gods would destroy the heaven and the earth. Qur'ān 21.22 reads: 'Were there gods in earth and heaven other than God, they would surely go to ruin' (tr. Arberry).[41] According to Ibn Taymiyya, one should consider the Qur'ān not only as a basis of information in religious matters but also as a source of rational proofs concerning God's existence, His unity, prophecy and the world to come.[42] This notion can be traced back to al-Ash'arī's *Risālat istiḥsān al-khawḍ fī 'ilm al-Kalām*,[43] and from him it might have reached al-Ghazālī who developed the idea in his *al-Qistās al-mustaqīm.* Al-Ghazālī's work might have influenced the traditionalist Mālikite scholar Abū Bakr Muḥammad ibn 'Abdallāh ibn al-'Arabī (d. 543/1148), who met al-Ghazālī and learned from him.[44] Answering the question relating to the excuse of scholars who deviate from the teachings of the Qur'ān and deal extensively and profoundly with rational proofs concerning the knowledge of God, Ibn al-'Arabī states that the Qur'ān includes rational proofs in a concise manner and in allusions. The Qur'ān sets forth the roots of rational proofs and not their branches and related topics. The function of extending and explaining these proofs and supplying their branches in a complete form is to be carried out by the scholars. The second excuse of the author is connected with polemics; the scholars wish to show to the unbelievers (*mulḥida*) and to the innovators (*mubtadi'a*) that the use of reason does not belong to them exclusively. The unbelievers and innovators are thus aware that they are refuted by means of every kind of argument.[45] Thus, according to the traditionalists, rational arguments constitute an integral part of the Qur'ān.

In sum, we have seen that reason plays an important role for the traditionalists, whether as a device for proving their tenets, or as a polemical tool. However, since reason was not the basis of traditionalism and because it served as the core of the teachings of their adversaries the rationalists, the traditionalists have criticised the use of rational arguments. How they have treated this issue is the subject matter of the next chapter.

3

TRADITIONALISM AGAINST RATIONALISM

THE TRADITIONALISTS' CRITICISM OF THE USE OF RATIONAL METHODS

Since our work treats Islamic thought as it appears mainly in theological treatises, works of *uṣūl* and creeds, it is not our specific aim to refer to other kinds of Islamic religious literature. However, we must bear in mind that some Muslim scholars have criticised the use of rational arguments in the interpretation of the Qur'ān.[1] They have prohibited the use of independent rational interpretation of the Qur'ān (*al-tafsīr bi'l-ra'y*).[2] A criticism of rational methods in the sphere of Islamic law is illustrated in the teachings of the Ẓāhirite school of law which rebuked the use of analogical reasoning (*qiyās*) in deriving law from the Qur'ān or the Sunna.[3] In both cases, the criticism was directed against the very use of rational arguments, not against their place in argumentation or interpretation.

As we have seen, the traditionalists' attitude towards rational arguments in theology is two-sided. On the one hand, rational proofs of the principles of religion, such as God's existence, His unity and attributes, are rejected by extreme traditionalists, but on the other, the traditionalists use rational arguments to prove principles derived from the Qur'ān and the Sunna and to refute their adversaries. They oppose the tenets of the rationalists derived from speculative considerations, and also the inevitable consequence of using reason, namely, the diversity of the rationalists' theological solutions, as against the uniformity of the traditionalists' teachings.

The foremost target of the traditionalists was the Mutakallimūn,[4] the main body of Muslim scholars (except for the philosophers who are not treated in this work), who used speculative ways of reasoning to formulate their theological tenets and also to attack the traditionalists' approaches. An early example of a traditionalist's criticism of rationalism is Ibn Qutayba's work *Ta'wīl mukhtalif al-ḥadīth*, which constitutes his response to the Mutakallimūn's criticism of the traditionists (*ahl al-ḥadīth*).[5] The core of the Mutakallimūn's criticism of the traditionists is the latter's transmission of contradictory traditions which brought about controversy in the Muslim community which in turn caused it to split into sects each claiming truth on the basis of traditions. Such sects are the Khārijites and their opponents the Murji'ites,[6] the Qadarites and their opponents the Jabrites,[7] the Rāfiḍites and their opponents.[8]

Ibn Qutayba levels the same accusation, but from another point of view; he blames the Mutakallimūn for introducing contradictory doctrines which are based on analogical reasoning and speculation. Abū al-Hudhayl al-ʿAllāf,[9] for example, opposes al-Naẓẓām's[10] doctrines, and al-Najjār[11] opposes both of them. They would have had an excuse, says Ibn Qutayba, if they had differed on juristic matters, but they differed on matters such as God's unity, His attributes and power and so on, which are known to a prophet only through revelation. Whereas, concerning the principles of religion, the traditionalists are in agreement – the only exception being the question of the reciting of the Qur'ān, whether it is created or uncreated – the Mutakallimūn are in disagreement.[12] Moreover, they sometimes ascribe contradictory statements to the Qur'ān, and state that it attests to these contradictions. ʿUbayd Allāh ibn al-Ḥasan, a governor of the district of al-Basra, said that whoever adhered to the doctrine of predestination was right, and whoever adhered to the doctrine of free will was also right, because both doctrines have their basis in the Qur'ān.[13] There are also extremely illogical teachings of the Mutakallimūn. Al-Bakr, the eponym of the Bakriyya sect, which is mentioned by al-Ashʿarī as one of the ten kinds of Muslims,[14] says that whoever steals a grain of mustard then dies without expressing repentance will suffer in Hell forever like Jews and Christians.[15]

The notion that reason is multi-faceted and that it leads to different directions also occurs in Ibn Qutayba's contemporary al-Dārimī (d. 280/893 or 282/895). According to al-Dārimī , the intelligible (*maʿqūl*) is not homogeneous. Each sect considers its ideas as intelligible and its opponents' ideas as unintelligible. Even in one and the same sect, says al-Dārimī directing his words to the Jahmiyya, there are many groups, each claiming that its thought is intelligible.[16] This phenomenon reminds one of the term *takāfu' al-adilla* (equality of [contradictory] proofs), which means that all speculation is futile.[17] Ibn Taymiyya explains this term in reference to the Mutakallimūn; what characterises them is arguments, contradictions and doubts which are directed against other Mutakallimūn.[18]

Ibn Taymiyya further develops the notion of the weakness of speculation by saying that rational arguments vary and are sometimes self-contradictory.

> The preference of rational arguments over traditional ones is impossible and unsound. As for the preference of the traditional proofs, it is possible and sound ... that is on account of the fact that being known through reason or not is not an inherent attribute (*ṣifa lāzima*) of a thing but rather a relative one (*min al-umūr al-nisbiyya al-iḍāfiyya*), for Zayd may know through his reason what Bakr does not know, and a man may know at a certain time through his reason what he will not know at another time.[19]

Thus reason is an unstable device, while tradition is stable and does not change. According to Ibn Taymiyya, scholars dispute with one another even concerning necessary knowledge which is supposed to be homogeneous.[20] There are many examples of the phenomenon that reason leads to a variety of opinions. Thus, the Muʿtazila and some of the Shīʿa who followed them have disputed with *ahl al-ithbāt* (those who affirm God's attributes and predetermination), each claiming that their respective tenets (the Muʿtazilite denial of attributes and predetermination counters the affirmation of attributes and predetermination by *ahl al-ithbāt*) are known through rational and decisive proofs (*adilla ʿaqliyya qaṭʿiyya*).[21]

> Moreover, the more remote a school is from Tradition the greater the dispute among them. Thus the Muʿtazilites have more debates among themselves than do the Mutakallimūn of *ahl al-ithbāt*. The Shīʿa exceeds the Muʿtazila in its internal disputes and the philosophers have the highest number of divergent opinions.[22]

'Ibn Taymiyya does not ignore the question which one would immediately raise, to the effect that the ancient scholars of Tradition (the *Ṣaḥāba* and the *Tābiʿūn*) also engaged in debates relating to religious issues so that they are not different from the Mutakallimūn of the Muʿtazila and of *ahl al-ithbāt* and so that Tradition, too, contains contradictory notions.[23] He says, however, that when these debates were taking place, the ancient scholars turned to God and to the Messenger in order to receive the right decision. Some of them were right, and as a result God made their reward greater, and others were mistaken in their striving for truth, and God forgave them. Answering, elsewhere, the question of how 'Ā'isha opposed two traditions of the Prophet through using Qur'ān verses, Ibn Taymiyya says: "We do not deny that they contradicted one text by another. We only deny that they contradicted the texts through their reason. The texts themselves do not contradict each other except for command and prohibition where one text is abrogative (*nāsikh*) and the other is abrogated (*mansūkh*). As for pieces of information (*akhbār*), it is inconceivable that they should contradict one another" (*Dar'*, vol. 5, p. 230f.). By *akhbār*, Ibn Taymiyya means non-practical doctrines like the question of attributes and predestination. In fine, Tradition contains the solution to the problem of self-contradiction; no external device should be used to solve it.'[24]

In addition to his preceding contention, Ibn Taymiyya states that traditional matters such as the affirmation of God's attributes and His predetermination, whose truth the rationalists contest, are known through necessary knowledge which ensues from the process of *tawātur*.[25] As a result of using *tawātur*, this knowledge cannot be false; moreover it is certain, contrary to the opponents' rational arguments which convey doubts and hence uncertainty.[26] It is to be noted that there are some other issues concerning which controversies arose, such as the traditional doctrine that the spirit was created before the body while, according to the Kalām, an accident, in this case the spirit, cannot exist without a substrate, namely, the body.[27]

Dealing with rational proofs leads not only to doubts and confusion, but also to a mixture of truth and falseness.[28] 'Those who oppose the Qur'ān and the Sunna through what they call rational proofs (*'aqliyyāt*), such as speculative proofs (*kalāmiyyāt*) and philosophical proofs (*falsafiyyāt*) and the like, base their doctrines only on general and ambiguous opinions which bear many meanings, and their ambiguity in form and sense requires them to also include truth and falseness.'[29] Ibn Taymiyya regards the mixture of truth and falseness as the origin of innovations (*mansha' al-bida'*), for if an innovation were totally false, this would be manifest and hence it would be rejected; and if, on the other hand, it were totally true, it would agree with Tradition, because Tradition does not contradict pure truth. An innovation combines both truth and falseness, and hence misleads people. Ibn Taymiyya explains that the ancient sages applied neither affirmation nor negation to the innovations, for these two devices would have applied to both truth and falseness.[30]

Ibn Taymiyya also rejects the technical terms used by the theologians and the philosophers. In their doctrines, they employ terms which do not belong to the pure Arabic of the Qur'ān, the Sunna and ordinary linguistic usage.[31] This is a part of the general contention according to which the Qur'ān and the Sunna did not order people to engage in Kalām and the ancients did not deal with it.[32]

One of the ways to fight against rationalism is to show the dangerous consequences of the preference of reason over revelation. This preference means that nothing can be learned from the Qur'ān and the Sunna, a notion which may cause unbelief and heresy.[33] Very probably following the Ḥanbalite scholar al-Barbahārī (d. 330/941), Ibn Taymiyya goes even further, saying that a deviation from revelation in one issue leads to total deviation.[34] Possibly, he alludes here to Mutakallimūn who preferred reason as a source of knowledge concerning some theological subjects such as God's attributes and predetermination, whereas on other issues they remained loyal to the doctrines of traditionalism. Two more evil results are indicated: speculation, as experience attests, does not bring about piety and indeed, those who engage in it are usually immoral;[35] and the preference of reason leads to considering the common people, who constitute the majority of the Muslims, unbelievers (*takfīr al-ʿawāmm*), for they know religion only through adhering to the teachings of the Qur'ān, the Sunna and their ancestors.[36]

Another main traditionalist target is the rationalists' figurative interpretation (*ta'wīl*) of the Qur'ān and the Sunna. The rationalists justify their use of this device by stating that without it the Qur'ān and the Sunna are full of anthropomorphisms[37] which debase the true perception of God as eternal being unlike any other being. It is not our aim here to elaborate on anthropomorphism, but rather to shed light on the reaction of the traditionalists to the method of *ta'wīl*. However, an example is needed to illustrate the problem. Let us put forth the famous verse in Qur'an 20.5 to which books and chapters were dedicated.[38] It reads: 'The All-Compassionate sat himself upon the Throne'. This verse was interpreted by the likeners (*mushabbihūn*) to mean that God's place is on the Throne. Following the Jahmites, the Muʿtazilites hold that God is everywhere, for if He were in a certain place, He would be limited as a body.[39] Most of the Muʿtazilites think that 'God is everywhere' means that He directs and rules (*istawā*, which literally means 'he sat', is figuratively interpreted by using the verb *istawlā*, meaning 'he ruled') every place.[40]

This kind of interpretation is vehemently attacked by the Ḥanbalite scholar Ibn Qudāma al-Maqdisī (d. 620/1223) on the strength of several arguments. The first argument is based on the famous verse (Qur'ān 3.7) which reads:

> It is He who brought down the Book; in it there are self-evident verses (*muḥkamāt*) that are the basis of the Book (*umm al-kitāb*) and others that are ambiguous (*mutashābihāt*). Those who deviate from the right way follow the ambiguous verses for the purpose of [bringing about] dissension and of interpreting them (*ta'wīlahu*, interpreting the ambiguous ones). Only God knows the interpretation of these verses (*wa-ma ya'lamu ta'wīlahu illa allāh*). And the most erudite persons (*al-rāsikhūn fi'l-'ilm*) say we believe in them (the ambiguous verses), each one (every ambiguous or self-evident verse) is from God, and only the clever people pay attention to [it].[41]

According to Ibn Qudāma, God rebukes both those who follow the *ta'wīl*, which for him is obviously a wrong interpretation, and those who strive for dissension. The two parties are accused of deviation, which proves that striving for such an interpretation is forbidden. Moreover, stating that 'only God knows the interpretation of these verses' means that God prevents them from attaining their aim. The following verse (3.8) 'Our God! Do not make our hearts deviate after You have guided us' shows that believers do not want to be like deviators who use the method of *ta'wīl*.[42]

According to the second argument, which is also known from other sources,[43] if *ta'wīl* had been obligatory on the Muslims, Muḥammad would have explained it, for a prophetic message should not come late. And also, the Prophet is not above the believers as far as carrying out laws (*al-aḥkām*) is concerned, so if *ta'wīl* had been obligatory on him, he would not have violated it. Muḥammad was ordered in Qur'ān 5.67 ('O Messenger, deliver what has been sent down to you from your Lord') to deliver every divine message to his community, hence it is inconceivable that he should have not done so.[44]

Thirdly, the method of the ancient scholars and the religious leaders who followed them (*a'imma*; he may mean by this term the heads of the juristic schools) with regard to anthropomorphisms was to affirm (*iqrār*) and accept them without interpretation or cancellation (*ta'ṭīl*). One must not oppose their way or deviate from it.

Fourthly, whoever uses figurative interpretation judges God through criteria which cannot be known by the interpreter. He interprets God's intention without knowing what God intends. According to Ibn Qudāma, the best argument the interpreter can put forth is that a certain word may be interpreted in a certain way. However, one cannot deduce from the mere fact that there is a possible interpretation that this is God's intention, for there are other possible interpretations some of which the interpreter, who is incapable of knowing all the meanings of a word, does not know. As a corroboration for this notion, Ibn Qudāma cites Qur'ān 7.33: 'God has forbidden ... to speak of Him what one does not know'.

The fifth argument shows that *ta'wīl* is an innovation in religion against which the Prophet has warned the Muslims. *Al-muta'awwil* (whoever interprets figuratively) renounces the Sunna of the Prophet and that of the Righteous Caliphs.

In the sixth argument, Ibn Qudama states that there is no need to exert efforts for the purpose of establishing this kind of interpretation, because no action is required by religion as a result of this interpretation. The believer must believe in the anthropomorphic words without knowing their meaning, just as he believes in God's angels without knowing their essence.[45] A similar argument was already adduced by al-Taymī, who states that the discussion of God's attributes is a branch of the discussion of God's essence. The affirmation of God's essence is an affirmation of existence (*ithbāt wujūd*), not modality (*ithbāt kayfiyya*). Likewise, the affirmation of God's attributes is also an affirmation of existence and not modality. On the question of how belief is valid when one does not know the real meaning of the object of one's belief, al-Taymī answers that belief is valid due to God's obligation on man to believe which man absolutely knows. God orders man to believe in His angels, Books, Messengers, the Last Day, Paradise and Hell, even if man does not know all the aspects of these objects.[46] According to al-Taymī, there is a prohibition to deal with the modality of God's attributes. This prohibition is expressed in the statement: 'God's unity should not be dealt with through analogy (*laysa al-tawḥīd bi'l-qiyās*)'. Al-Taymī buttresses this statement by referring to the fact that when God describes Himself in the Qur'ān, He does not set forth the causes of His attributes; God does not say, 'I know because of such and such a cause'.[47] Therefore, analogy should not be used in this issue.[48]

In the seventh argument, Ibn Qudma uses the method of *qisma*.[49] Let us suppose, he says, that the *ta'wīl* is obligatory. In such a case, there must be two possibilities; it is obligatory either on all the people (*al-a'yān*) or on whoever has a proof for it. The first possibility, namely, the obligation to use *ta'wīl* without knowing its proof, means that God requires man to believe in ignorance (*taklīf al-qawl bi'l-jahl*), which is forbidden by consensus. If it is not obligatory on whoever does not know its proof, how do those who adhere to it order the masses (*al-'āmma*) and those who do not know its proofs to use it?

Ibn Qudāma regards *ta'wīl* as a part of the method of individual interpretation (*al-ra'y*). Since this method is forbidden, *ta'wīl* is also forbidden. In its kind, this argument (the eighth) is like the fifth, which considers *ta'wīl* a part of the general group of innovations.

The ninth argument is as follows. Whoever uses *ta'wīl* (*al-muta'awwil*) combines two procedures: (1) he describes God through an attribute which God does not use to describe Himself; and (2) he denies an attribute of God which God ascribes to Himself. For example, if he says that the meaning of *istawā* (sat Himself on the Throne: Qur'ān 20.5) is 'He ruled', he describes God through an attribute which God does not use to describe Himself, and he denies of Him an attribute (*istiwā'*) which occurs seven times in the Qur'ān. Could not God, Ibn Qudāma asks ironically, say *istawlā* (if He really wanted to say this word)?[50]

Ibn Qudāma also criticises the Mutakallimūn for using the method of *al-istidlāl bi'l-shāhid 'alā al-ghā'ib* (literally 'inferring what is absent from what is present').[51] He introduces the Kalām device as follows: 'What is absent (*al-ghā'ib*) is like what is proved (*thabata*) with regard to us (*fī ḥaqqinā*)',[52] meaning that which is true concerning man is also true concerning God. For the refutation of this method, Ibn Qudāma set forth three arguments: (1) the Mutakallimūn name God absent, whereas His names and attributes appear in the Qur'ān. Did the Mutakallimūn, asks Ibn Qudāma sarcastically, not find a name for God out of His ninety-nine names, so that they had to use another name?[53] Moreover, God has denied this name of Himself, saying: 'We were not absent' (Qur'ān 7.7).[54]

(2) The Mutakallimūn are accused of *tashbīh*, for their method of *istidlāl* likens God's names and attributes to man's names and attributes, and this is the essence of *tashbīh*.

(3) This argument is an elaboration of the second one. The Mutakallimūn affirm God's other attributes, such as hearing, seeing, knowledge and life. Now, using the method of *istidlāl* means

that God hears, sees, knows and lives through instruments, just as man carries out these actions through instruments (organs, and body in the case of life). Consequently, God is likened to His creation, a notion rejected by the Mutakallimūn. Ibn Qudāma employs here the Kalām method of *ilzām* which means forcing the imaginary opponent to admit views which are absurd or heretical, or contrary to the opponent's own views. It is carried out through inferring conclusions from the opponent's opinions.[55] In the present argument, the basis is the opponent's method of *istidlāl* which is exploited to refute the Mutakallimūn's rejection of *tashbīh*; this procedure finally leads to the conclusion that the Mutakallimūn hold *tashbīh*. Ibn Qudāma, who vehemently attacks the Mutakallimūn, uses their method in order to render their thesis untenable.

THE ATTITUDE TOWARDS THE KALĀM AND THE MUTAKALLIMŪN

The attitude of the traditionalists towards the rationalists, mainly the Mutakallimūn, follows two principles: prohibition against engaging in Kalām, including breaking off relations with and excommunication of the Mutakallimūn; and refutation of their tenets. These principles are expressed in different ways. Al-Suyūṭī banned discussion of Kalām issues, for debate causes controversies and innovations in religion. He compared his prohibition to the prohibition against dealing with the ambiguous verses of the Qur'ān.[56] Basing himself on ʿAbdallāh ibn Muḥammad al-Harawī's (d. 481/1089) *Dhamm al-kalām wa-ahlihi*, al-Suyūṭī points out that the hostile attitude towards the Kalām and the Mutakallimūn is not characteristic only of one generation. Indeed, it has accompanied all the generations beginning with the *Ṣaḥāba* and ending with scholars of the fifth/eleventh century, including (it could not be otherwise) the imams of the great schools of law.[57] As we have seen elsewhere, it is typical of the traditionalists to strengthen their views through relying on the overwhelming majority of the Muslims.

In a work entitled *Akhbār ʿAmr ibn ʿUbayd*[58] written by the Shāfiʿite traditionist and lexicographer ʿAlī ibn ʿUmar al-Dāraquṭnī (d. 385/995), it is related that the son of the famous Baṣran traditionist Yūnus ibn ʿUbayd (d. 139/756 or 140/757; see the German text, p. 25) violated his father's prohibition against visiting the Muʿtazilite Mutakallim ʿAmr ibn ʿUbayd (d. 144/761). Yūnus ibn ʿUbayd's reaction to his son's visit was that it is better to meet God (that is, on the Day of Judgement) with grave sins such as fornication, theft and drinking wine than to meet Him with the views of ʿAmr ibn ʿUbayd and his followers.[59] This anecdote demonstrates the bitter hostility of the traditionalists towards the rationalists. Yūnus ibn ʿUbayd seems to have regarded ʿAmr ibn ʿUbayd as a great threat to religion, because of his attitude towards the *ḥadīth* (he lied concerning traditions) and his belief in free will.[60]

Sometimes the breaking-off of relations with the rationalists has taken the form of prohibitions against praying behind them (a Jahmite, for example, should not serve as an imam in a prayer) or marrying them.[61]

In his *al-Iʿtiqād wa'l-hidāya ilā sabīl al-rashād ʿalā madhhab al-salaf wa-aṣḥāb al-ḥadīth*, the Shāfiʿite scholar al-Bayhaqī (d. 458/1065) devotes a chapter to the prohibition against sitting in the company of the people of innovations (*al-nafy ʿan mujālasat ahl al-bidaʿ*). The bitterest attack in this chapter is reserved for those people who believe in free will (*al-qadariyya*).[62] He seems to refer to the Muʿtazilites and not to the early believers in free will, who are also called *qadariyya*. Probably, beginning from the ninth century, *qadariyya* had become a pejorative name for the Muʿtazila.[63] Let us cite, for example, three traditions: (1) 'Do not sit with the people of *qadar* and do not open conversation with them';[64] (2) 'The *qadariyya* are the Zoroastrians (*majūs*)[65] of this community – when they are ill, do not visit them, and when they die, do not attend their funeral'; (3) 'Two groups of my community have no connection to Islam: the *murji'a*[66] and the *qadariyya*'. The last two traditions point out a tendency to excommunicate the rationalists, or those who do not adhere to the Qur'ān and the Sunna, from the legitimate community. This phenomenon of excommunication or declaring the ideological opponent to be an unbeliever (*takfīr*) is a common method. Thus the Shāfiʿite scholar al-Shirāzī (d. 476/1083) declares whoever denies the Ashʿarite doctrines to be an unbeliever.[67] When the Muʿtazilite scholar Ḥafṣ al-Fard (fl. the first half of the third/eighth century)[68] said that the Qur'ān was created, al-Shāfiʿī said to him: 'You have disbelieved in the Mighty God'.[69] According to the Ḥanafite scholar Abū Yūsuf al-Anṣārī (d. 182/798), who was the most distinguished of Abū Ḥanīfa's disciples, knowledge through speculative theology (*kalām*) is ignorance, and ignorance of Kalām is knowledge. Whoever becomes a master of Kalām is accused of heresy (*zandaqa*).[70] Al-Shāfiʿī's attitude towards the Mutakallimūn was no less severe. His judgement of them is that they should be smitten with palm branches and shoes in the presence of many people and then it will be said: this is the punishment of those who abandoned the Qur'ān and the Sunna and turned to the Kalām.[71] However, as attested in the Shāfi'ite scholar al-Ḥusayn ibn Mas'ūd al-Baghawī (d. 516/1122),[72] the attitude towards the sectarians (*ahl al-ahwā'*) depends sometimes on their doctrines. The traditionist Abū Sulaymān Aḥmad ibn Muḥammad al-Bustī al-Khaṭṭābī (d. 388/998)[73] did not call the sectarians who interpreted the Qur'ān and made mistakes unbelievers, and he also allowed their testimony to be accepted[74] as long as they did not call Muhammad's Companions unbelievers. 'Abd Allāh ibn Aḥmad ibn Ḥanbal related in the name of his father that one should not pray behind whoever held the createdness of the Qur'ān.[75] Again, it should be noted that when speaking of the people of innovations (*ahl al-bida'*) or of the sectarians (*ahl al-ahwā'*), the scholars do not always mean to speak of those who hold rational doctrines, for these appellations also refer to the possessors of mystical or political notions and to performers of unusual practices. The different kinds of attitude seem to refer to all kinds of heretics, the rationalists occupying a central place among them.

Another important note is the fact that the Qur'ān contains many verses in which the word *hawan* (literally 'passion') occurs. These verses are exploited for the purpose of refuting the sectarians (*ahl al-ahwā'*), for example Qur'ān 18.28 'Do not obey one whose heart We have made neglectful of Our remembrance so that he follows his passion' (or his sectarian doctrine, *hawāhu*).[76]

The rationalists are described, along with despotic kings (*mulūk jā'ira*) and ignorant ascetics (*juhhāl al-mutaṣawwifa*), as those who corrupt religion. They are evil scholars (*aḥbār sū'*), who deviate from religion through their views and untrue analogies which permit what God forbids and forbid what God permits.[77]

In al-Taymī there exists even the notion, which I have not seen elsewhere, that the Mutakallimūn are not religious scholars (*'ulamā'*). Basing himself on the ancient scholars (*'ulamā' al-salaf*), al-Taymī states that, in order to justify his position, a religious leader (*imām fī'l-dīn*) must have the following characteristics: he must know the language of the Arabs with all its divergencies,[78] the different views of the religious scholars, the rules of grammar, the Qur'ān, its interpretations, its different recitations and several issues relating to the Qur'ān, such as the self-evident and ambiguous verses, and he must know the Traditions and their kinds. Moreover, he must be a pious man. Whoever has these properties may be the originator of a religious system (*madhhab*). Taking into account these conditions, al-Taymī draws the conclusion that those who built their methods on their intellect, such as the Muʿtazilites Abū ʿAlī al-Jubbā'ī (d. 303/915), his son Abū Hāshim al-Jubbā'ī (d. 321/933), Abū al-Qāsim al-Kaʿbī (d. 319/931), al-Naẓẓām (d. 221/836 or 231/845), the Murji'ite Mutakallim al-Ḥusayn ibn Muḥammad al-Najjār (d. 221/836?), and the Mutakallim Ibn Kullāb (d. 241/855), are not learned men like Muḥammad's Companions and their Followers. Furthermore, one cannot place them in the rank of either juristic scholars like al-Shāfiʿī (d. 205/820) or scholars of language like al-Aṣmaʿī (d. 215/830), or grammarians like al-Khalīl ibn Aḥmad (d. c. 170/786), or those who are well versed in the sciences of the Qur'ān like Nāfiʿ ibn ʿAbd al-Raḥmān (d. 170/786), or traditionists like Aḥmad ibn Ḥanbal (d. 241/855), or ascetics like al-Ḥasan al-Baṣrī (d. 110/728). Al-Taymī concludes this section by saying that the worst method, adopted by people who believe in reason (*ahl al-qawl bi'l-ʿaql*), is to abandon the Qur'ān and the Sunna and the statements of the Companions and the scholars who followed them.[79]

In spite of al-Taymī's severe attitude towards the rationalists, whom he does not consider real scholars, he presents a response of Abū Sulaymān Aḥmad ibn Muḥammad al-Khaṭṭābī to a certain scholar, who apparently asked how one should deal with the Mutakallimūn. Through this response, we understand that the scholar vacillated between quitting the Mutakallimūn and sitting with them. Either alternative presented a dilemma. On the one hand, the scholar might have succumbed to their claims, and on the other, he might have disputed with them and rejected their stands. Again, both possibilities seemed to him difficult; if he wanted to accept their views, religion would prevent him from doing so, and if he wanted to refute them, he would have to use rational arguments, for they were not persuaded by the plain texts. Therefore, this unknown scholar asked al-Khaṭṭābī to supply him with proofs and arguments which could not rationally be refuted by the Mutakallimūn. He made his decision to refute the Mutakallimūn, and not just to break off relations with them as some other authorities had recommended.[80]

Al-Khaṭṭābī says that this dissension, meaning the Kalām, has spread all over the country, and only one whom God protected from it would be safe. He asks himself the reason for the success of the Kalām. And he answers that it is the seduction of the Devil which made people deviate from the path of the Qur'ān and the

Sunna. The Devil caused the clever people to think that if they were content with the teachings of the Qur'ān and the Sunna and accepted their plain meanings, they would be like the masses (*al-'āmma*), which means, naturally, degradation. As a result, they began to deal with speculative theology in order to distinguish themselves from the masses.[81] Another reason for the strengthening of the Kalām was the weakness of the belief in finding the truth in the Qur'ān and the Sunna, which in turn caused the unbelievers to attack Islam on the basis of unsound arguments. The Muslims thought that only a reaction through speculative means would overcome their opponents, a thought which proved to be a grave error.[82] Al-Khaṭṭābī accuses the Mutakallimūn of taking their doctrines from the philosophers, who were obliged to turn to these doctrines, because they did not affirm the prophecies.[83] Whoever accepts Muhammad's prophecy needs no speculative methods, for prophecy contains what man must know concerning religion.[84]

In sum, there are divergent attitudes towards the rationalists in Islamic theological literature. These attitudes range from total rejection and excommunication to permission to debate with them. The Ḥanbalites do not appear as the sole extremists in this issue; traditionalism in its different forms again exists in all Islamic schools of law. When al-Suyūṭī defames the Kalām in his *Ṣawn*, he uses the writings of scholars from various schools, Ḥanbalites (al-Harawī), Shāfi'ites (al-Muḥāsibī), Mālikites (Abū Ṭālib al-Makkī) and Ibn Jarīr al-Ṭabarī, who established his own school of law.

4

THE FOUNDATIONS OF RATIONALISM

As pointed out in the Introduction, pure rationalism does not exist in Islamic theology. Concerning this field, we can speak only of rationalist tendencies, and the terms 'rationalist' and 'rationalism' are rightly used only with reference to some theological issues. However, since there are ingredients of rationalism in Islamic theology, I prefer to use this term. The Muʿtazilites were very close to such rationalism in some of their tenets, but their religiosity cannot be denied, because revelation was a central issue for them. Scholars like Ibn al-Rāwandī (see below) who took the Muʿtazilite notions to their extremes, that is, the consideration of the intellect as the source of all knowledge, became unbelievers.

The basis of rationalism is the notion that God and the world can be perceived through the intellect which God creates in man. Concerning God, this perception means that God's existence, His unity and His attributes can be known through reason. Concerning the world, it means that the creation of the world and its structure, man and his actions can be logically understood. From this foundation, it follows that the world is directed according to rational rules and that, hence, even God is subject to these rules. We shall immediately see that according to some Muʿtazilites, God is logically obliged to act in a certain manner. It is no wonder, thus, that God's first obligation on man is to speculate (or reflect) in order to attain the knowledge of God (*al-naẓar al-mu'addī ilā ma'rifat allāh*).[1] Contrary to the view of the traditionalists, one can know God without the support of the Scripture, and even without a teacher.[2] However, the motive which causes man to reflect is a warning (*khāṭir*) made by God to the effect that if he does not reflect, he will be punished.[3] In *Sharḥ al-uṣūl al-khamsa*,[4] Mānakdīm states that 'the knowledge of God is attained only through rational proofs' (*ma'rifat allāh ta'ālā lā tunālu illā bi-ḥujjat al-'aql*). He mentions four kinds of proofs: (1) the rational proof; (2) the Book, that is, the Qur'ān; (3) the Sunna; and (4) the Consensus (*al-ijmā'*). Now, the knowledge of God cannot be obtained through the last three proofs, since they are the branches (*furū'*) of the knowledge of God, and it is inconceivable to use the branches in order to affirm the existence of the root (*aṣl*). The Qur'ān, says Mānakdīm, is approved as a proof only when one proves that it is a just and wise speech, and this derives from the knowledge of God, His unity and justice.[5]

Another foundation of Islamic rationalism is the overwhelming power of reason over revelation. Since reason is the governing principle of the world, the contradiction between revelation and reason must be solved according to reason. For example, anthropomorphisms in the Qur'ān and the Sunna should be interpreted in a figurative way, otherwise God loses His attributes of being the Creator and the Everlasting; if God is like the created things, He can be neither the Creator nor the Everlasting.

It is not our aim in this treatise to deal with the rationalists' proofs of creation and God's existence, or to consider their advantages and disadvantages from the point of view of reason,[6] but some examples are needed to illustrate their activity. Early on, two Mu'tazilite theologians, al-Iskāfī (d. 240/854) and al-Naẓẓām (d. 221/836 or 231/845), used the proof for creation from the impossibility of an infinite number: 'The world must have a beginning since an infinite past time could not have been traversed'.[7]

The proof from accidents is the standard Kalām proof for the creation of the world. Its basis is the structure of the world as seen by the Mutakallimūn. According to them, there are two elements which compose each body: (1) atom (*jawhar*, pl. *jawāhir* or *al-juz' allazī lā yatajazz'u*, an indivisible particle), an unchanging particle devoid of properties; and (2) accident (*'araḍ*, pl. *a'rāḍ*), the changeable element of each body, which comes into existence and disappears, like motion and rest in a body. Each existent body is composed of atoms and accidents. Since accidents come into existence and are necessarily parts of the body, the body also comes into existence. The universe is a body, hence it also came into existence. Abū al-Hudhayl al-'Allāf (d. 235/849) is said to have been the first Mu'tazilite Mutakallim who put forth this argument.[8] Other arguments for creation and God's existence are the argument from composition,[9] the argument from particularisation[10] and the argument from design.[11]

Basically, there is no difference between the Mu'tazilite and the Ash'arite Mutakallimūn in introducing rational proofs for creation and for God's existence. As a rule, Ash'arite Kalām manuals begin with a chapter on the sources of knowledge, then comes a chapter on proving the creation of the world and God's existence.[12] The difference lies in their treatment of the obligation to rationally know God's existence and the creation of the world. Al-Ash'arī holds that this obligation derives from revelation,[13] whereas the Mu'tazilites and even some of the Ash'arites, such as al-Qalānisī (d. 359/970) and his followers, regard this obligation as stemming from reason.[14]

The Mu'tazilites derive God's attribute of His being powerful (*qādir*) directly from His being the Creator of the world (*al-muḥdith li'l-'ālam*), for the possibility of one's being an agent (literally, one for whom an act is possible – *ṣaḥḥa minhu al-fi'l*) proves one's ability.[15] Likewise, His being knowing (*'ālim*) stems from the possibility of His carrying out perfect actions.[16] The combination of the two previous attributes brings about the third attribute, namely, His being the living (*ḥayy*). Whoever is powerful and knowing must be living.[17] Here the author uses the rational method mentioned above of proving what is absent from what is present (*al-istidlāl bi'l-shāhid 'alā al-ghā'ib*; see above, p. 26). The same method is used by the Ash'arite Mutakallimūn[18] but is rejected by the traditionalists, who learn God's attributes from the Qur'ān and the Sunna.[19]

A point of dispute between the Mu'tazilites and the Ash'arites was the relationship of God's attributes to His essence. The Mu'tazilites argued that whatever is eternal must be God and that God's unity denies multiplicity of attributes in Him, even though these attributes are eternally united in God and not separated in Him.[20] Thus they denied the real existence of attributes as separate spiritual entities in God. God is knowing (*'ālim*), powerful (*qādir*) and living (*ḥayy*) not by virtue of knowledge, power and life inhering in Him, as the Ash'arites thought, but by virtue of His essence. The Mu'tazilites represent here a clear rational consideration in denying the attributes as separate entities inhering in God.[21] On the other hand, the Ash'arites, owing to their commitment to the traditional tenets,[22] claimed that God is knowing by virtue of knowledge, but having been aware of God's unity and eternity, they also claimed that these attributes are neither identical with nor other than God. By stating that the attributes are not identical with God they, besides stressing the attributes' independent status as opposed to the Mu'tazilite stand, did not infringe on God's unity and eternity, and by stating that His attributes are not other than Him, they claimed that they inhered in Him. Thus the Ash'arites used reason in order to defend traditional views.

The discussion on free will and predestination supplies us with another example of rationalism in Islamic theology. In the range of our work it is impossible to set forth even a limited exposition of the history of the debate and its various arguments, therefore we shall only give the principles. According to the Mu'tazilites, man is free to choose his acts and he is capable of carrying them out due to the power that God grants him before he acts. They hold that 'ought implies can'; if God had predetermined a man to be an unbeliever and then ordered him to be a believer and punished him on account of his unbelief, He would have been unjust and irrational, because after having been predetermined to unbelief a man cannot be a believer. Here again, we see that the Mu'tazilites judge God in keeping with their rational understanding. The principle which applies to man applies also to God.[23]

In contrast, the Ash'arite point of departure is different; it is God's omnipotence. Since God creates all things, He also creates man's acts. To safeguard both man's responsibility and God's omnipotence, al-Ash'arī developed the theory of *kasb* (literally 'acquisition'), whereby God creates man's actions and as man appropriates them, he becomes responsible for them. How man can be responsible for an action for which God creates the power and also the power of appropriation is a question which al-Ash'arī and his followers tried to answer.[24] The theory of *kasb* was a rational attempt to harmonise the rational requisite of free will and the traditional dogma of predestination whether this dogma derives from the sacred texts or from the people's mentality. For other attempts at harmonisation, see Chapter 6. What is important in this context is that the Kalām theory of *kasb* penetrated into traditionalist circles. In his interpretation of *al-'aqīda al-taḥāwiyya*, whose author the Ḥanafite Abū Ja'far Aḥmad ibn Muḥammad al-Ṭaḥāwī (d. 322/933) says that 'man's actions are God's creation and man's appropriation' (*af'āl al-'ibād khalq allāh wa-kasb min al-'ibād*), the Ḥanafite scholar Ibn Abī al-'Izz (d. 792/1389), who is an example of traditionalism in Ḥanafism, adopted this theory.[25] Elsewhere, we see that although this scholar criticises the Kalām,[26] he uses a Kalām argument – the argument from hypothetical mutual prevention (*dalīl al-tamānu'*) – to demonstrate God's unity.[27] The core of this argument is the hypothesis that two producers cannot act harmoniously, and that inability or weakness is necessarily attached to one or to both of them. The argument has its basis in the Qur'ān (23.91, 21.22), but owes its elaboration to the Mutakallimūn.[28]

The Muʿtazilites hold that man understands what is good and what is evil through his own intelligence, which can intuit these values. Good and evil actions have intrinsic properties which can necessarily be known through man's reason. God reveals to man what he generally knows and also supplies him with the details of his obligations.[29] Contrary to this view, the Ashʿarites hold divine subjectivism: to wit, what God forbids is evil and what He orders is good. Thus man cannot know by his reason before revelation the ethical values. And also, God is not subject to the reasonable rules which man understands.[30] That God, in the rationalists' view, is subject to such rules is exemplified once more in the issue of God's assistance (*luf*). The Muʿtazilites think that man knows that God created him purposefully, that is, to benefit him.[31] If God had created man purposelessly, His creation would not have been wise. A purposeless act (*ʿabath*) is considered an act performed unwisely, and it is inconceivable to speak of God as unwise. The best benefit that God can give man is a reward obtained only through carrying out duties which God imposes on him. Two conditions are required for man to perform his duties in order to obtain reward: he must have the power to do them; and he must freely choose his acts, and his choice requires different motivations or rational alternatives. God must give man the power to act (*tamkīn*) and the motivation to do good deeds. This last assistance is called *luṭf*. If He did not do this, He would be unjust, which according to ʿAbd al-Jabbār corresponds to his being irrational.[32] The pains caused by God raise doubts about God's justice. The Muʿtazilites solve this problem by stating that pains caused by God benefit man. When God inflicts pains on man for the latter's benefit, He must give him compensation (*ʿiwaḍ*) which exceeds the measure of the pains.[33] Again, we see that, according to the Muʿtazilites, God does not act arbitrarily, but rather in keeping with reasonable rules which man can understand.[34] In contrast, the Ashʿarite doctrine does not impose any rules on God. According to them, God can inflict pains on man as He pleases without bestowing benefit or compensation.[35] We see thus that the Muʿtazilites are more rationalist than the Ashʿarites.

The discussion of the proofs for the trustworthiness of prophethood can also be carried out according to either the traditional or the rational line. This can be best shown through examining a passage in a treatise of the Ashʿarite scholar Fakhr al-Dīn al-Rāzī (d. 606/1210) entitled *al-nubuwwāt wa-mā yataʿallaqu bi-hā* (Prophecies and Pertinent Issues). The believers in prophethood, says al-Rāzī, are divided into two parties. The first are those who state that the miracles prove the prophet's trustworthiness.[36] After they know that the prophet is trustworthy, they know, through the prophet's sayings, truth and falsehood. This is the traditional method which was adopted by most religious people. The second party are those who first know the true dogmas and the right actions to which man must adhere. Then, when they see a man who calls people to these ideas and actions, and his call exercises a strong influence over the people leading them from falsehood to truth, they know that he is a true prophet who must be followed. According to al-Rāzī, this method of identifying the true prophet is logical and has very few doubts. It is based on several premises: (1) Man's perfection (*kamāl*) lies in knowing the truth in itself and goodness in order to carry out good actions. In other words, al-Rāzī speaks here of theoretical and practical perfections which are, of course, reminiscent of the philosophers' view concerning the rank of the philosopher. (2) People are divided into three groups concerning perfection and imperfection in theoretical and practical powers. Most people are imperfect in their theoretical and practical powers. There are some individuals whom al-Rāzī calls 'saints' (*awliyā'*), who are perfect in both domains, but they cannot cure the imperfect, namely, they cannot render them perfect. The last party are both perfect and capable of making the imperfect perfect – those are the prophets. (3) It is necessarily known that the degrees of perfection, from the point of view of number and force, are infinite. (4) Although imperfection is a general phenomenon among people, there must be among them a perfect person. This premise is proved through examining the different kinds of animals and people. (5) The perfect man occupies the highest rank of humanity which has a connection to the last rank of the angels.[37] In sum, in al-Rāzī's view, the knowledge of the theoretical and practical perfections precedes the knowledge of the true prophet.[38] Thus al-Rāzī comes very close to the philosophers' view.[39] However, he devotes a chapter[40] to proving that this method, by which while the branch is prophethood the root is metaphysics, is clearly attested in the Qur'ān. The course of Qur'ān 87 (*sūrat al-a'lā*), which begins with the mention of God and His actions in the world and continues with the characteristics of the Prophet and his mission, serves al-Rāzī as proof of his view. However, it is evident that the Qur'ān here is a corroboration for al-Rāzī's thesis which occurs first, and not the basis of his theory. Thus, he proves to be a rationalist concerning this issue. Al-Rāzī prefers this way of proving prophethood to proofs according to miracles, and regards it as the best way.[41] This view is characteristic of al-Rāzī's later works (*al-Maṭālib al-ʿāliya min al-ʿilm al-ilāhī, Maʿālim uṣūl al-dīn* and *al-Tafsīr al-kabīr* (known also as *Mafātīḥ al-ghayb*)), but in his *Muḥaṣṣal afkār al-mutaqaddimīn wa'l-muta'akhkhirīn* he still considers this proof as equivalent to the traditional proofs.[42] We see thus that in this issue an Ashʿarite theologian accepts the notion that one should deal with metaphysics before entering into religious matters. Al-Rāzī is an excellent example of a theologian who on a specific issue becomes a rationalist after being a traditionalist on the same issue. This proves again that in Islamic theology the term 'rationalist' should be used only with regard to specific issues and relatively.

It is common knowledge that the philosophers, since they deem resurrection of the body to be impossible,[43] consider the phenomena of the world to come symbols which aim at the education of the ordinary people. It is relevant to our inquiry to examine how rational considerations formulate the rationalists' attitude towards such phenomena.

ʿAdhāb al-qabr (the Punishment of the Grave) may serve as an example of the rationalists' attitude towards a dogma, the belief in which is obligatory according to the traditionalists.[44] According to this dogma, two angels called *munkar* and *nakīr* (literally 'the unknown angels' or 'the detestable angels')[45] ask a man who died about his beliefs and deeds in this world. If it is evident after the angels' interrogation that a man did not believe or that he committed grave sins, he will be punished in the grave. Some Muʿtazilites (ʿAmr ibn Ubayd (d. 200/815) was among them)[46] denied *ʿadhāb al-qabr* on the grounds that if it really took place, one would see the signs of torment in the dead person or hear his voice. That we do not see such signs proves that this dogma has no basis.[47] Rationalism here takes the form of necessary knowledge, that is, experience attested by one's seeing does not prove this phenomenon. Although Mānakdīm affirms *ʿadhāb al-qabr* on the basis of the Qur'ān and the Sunna,[48] he introduces modifications into the modality (*kayfiyya*) of its occurrence so as to render it reasonable. 'Know that if God wills to torment them, He must make them live, since tormenting an inanimate being (*jamād*) is absurd (*muḥāl*).'[49] Mānakdīm continues his thread of thought and states that just as it is incumbent on God to create life in order to torment man, so it is incumbent on Him to create intelligence in man so that the torment becomes positive, otherwise the tormented person will think that he is wronged (*maẓlūm*). It is to be noted that one needs intelligence also to know that one is being ill-treated. This is the reason why the people who are in Hell must also have intelligence.[50] Again we see that rational procedure as understood by man obliges God. God is restricted in His actions to a natural (= rational) sequence of actions. It is very probable that Mānakdīm also refutes the voluntaristic occasionalism held by some Mutakallimūn who assert that power, knowledge, hearing and seeing may inhere in a dead body.[51]

Rational considerations are not absent from the discussion of the Balance (*al-mīzān*). The Balance which will weigh man's deeds in the Day of Resurrection is plainly mentioned in the Qur'ān (see, for example, Qur'ān 21.47: 'And We shall set up the just balances [*al-mawāzīn al-qisṭ*] for the Resurrection'[52]). First, Mānakdīm states that the Qur'ān speaks here and elsewhere of a real balance. Then, asked how man's deeds can be weighed while they are accidents which cannot be weighed, he answers that it is possible that light represents obedience and darkness is a sign of transgression, and God puts both of them on the scales and weighs them.[53] It is also possible that God puts man's deeds in leaves and weighs the leaves.[54] This solution is mentioned in al-Baghdādī's *Uṣūl* (p. 246) as a rational way which is stated in traditions. Such possibilities seem very odd to the modern reader, but seem to have been reasonable in the eyes of the rationalist Muslim of the eleventh century.

Another example of the Resurrection phenomena is the Path (*ṣirāṭ*) which leads to Paradise. The Path occurs many times in the Qur'ān (for example Qur'ān 37.23: 'Guide them to the Path of Hell'). According to the Sunna, the Path is finer than a hair and sharper than a sword. Whoever was righteous would cross the Path and enter Paradise, but whoever was wicked would stumble and fall into Hell.[55] Mānakdīm rejects this description of the Path, which he ascribes to the *ḥashwiyya*,[56] on the grounds that the Hereafter is not a place of imposition of duties. Therefore God will not inflict the crossing of the Path on man. Moreover, the Path is a way, while the above-mentioned description has no connection to a way. Mānakdīm says that 'Abd al-Jabbār relates in his book (probably Mānakdīm means 'Abd al-Jabbār's *Sharḥ al-uṣūl al-khamsa*) that many Mu'tazilite scholars hold that the Path consists of the signs which show the acts of obedience and the acts of transgression; whoever adheres to the former is brought to Paradise and whoever adheres to the latter is brought to Hell. Mānakdīm does not accept this interpretation either. According to him, there is no compelling reason to cancel the plain meaning (*ẓāhir*) of the Path and to interpret it figuratively. Thus, surprisingly enough and contrary to ʿAbd al-Jabbār, Mānakdīm accepts the notion of *bi-lā kayfa*; he accepts that this is a path, but denies the literal meaning of the Path and does not put forth any positive interpretation.[57] It is very interesting that a Muʿtazilite thinker adopts an Ashʿarite solution to the problem of anthropomorphism. Thus, just as rationalist notions penetrated traditional circles, traditional theories found their way into the rationalist circles. The ideological boundaries of the schools of thought have not always remained closed.

5

THE RATIONALISTS' CRITICISM OF TRADITIONALISM

Apart from rationalist opposition to some traditionalist theological tenets, there exists criticism of the fundamentals of the traditionalists' theology and their practices. This criticism can be divided into five parts: (1) criticism of the Qur'ān; (2) criticism of the *ḥadīth*; (3) criticism of the ancient scholars (*al-salaf*); (4) criticism of the Consensus; and (5) criticism of rituals and commandments. The criticism of religion and prophecy in general does not concern us here – although it is an interesting phenomenon which has been dealt with by Muslim theologians – since the holders of such views were few. They were considered to be unbelievers and had little influence on the debate between rationalism and traditionalism within Islam. The marginal contribution of those unbelievers to our topic was only the extension and refinement of the arguments in favour of prophecy.[1] As a rule, theological manuals refute the denial of prophecy through setting forth different rational arguments. For example, answering the claim that it is impossible for God to choose one person to be a prophet among others who equal him, al-Bāqillānī uses the method of *al-istidlāl bi'l-shāhid 'alā al-ghā'ib*, saying that it is possible for God to do this, just as a man may choose one of his friends over others who equal him.[2]

As for the Qur'ān, owing to its divine source, the rationalists, generally, have not criticised the text itself, but only such interpretations which do not agree with reason, for example the literal interpretation of anthropomorphic expressions, the statement that God knows by virtue of knowledge inhering in Him. However, in Ibn Ḥanbal's *al-Radd 'alā al-zanādiqa wa'l-jahmiyya* there occurs a criticism of the Qur'ān levelled by the *zanādiqa*.[3] If we understand by the term *zanādiqa* the Mu'tazilites, then we have here a rationalist criticism of the Qur'ān within Islam; this seems probable with the qualification that it derives from a bitter opponent of the Mu'tazila such as Ibn Ḥanbal. The main argument which occurs here is the self-contradictory nature of the Qur'ān. In many issues, the Qur'ān teaches contradictory ideas; for example, on the one hand it teaches that people will see God (Qur'ān 75.22–3) and on the other it teaches that man cannot see God (Qur'ān 6.103). We have found elsewhere other corroboration for a similar Mu'tazilite criticism (see above, Chapter 3, n. 13). However, it is also possible to regard the *zanādiqa* occurring in this text as people outside Islam who attacked the Qur'ān, or as Mu'tazilite theologians who became infidels, such as Ibn al-Rāwandī who censures the Qur'an in his *Kitāb al-dāmigh.*[4] As a rule, the Qur'ān was accepted by all parties, including the sectarians, as God's revelation. The case is different with regard to traditions. The rationalists did not and could not reject the Prophet's sayings, but had doubts concerning the authenticity of most of the traditions.[5]

The rationalists' criticism of the *ḥadīth* can be best drawn from Ibn Qutayba's *ta'wīl mukhtalif al-ḥadīth.* As we have seen, this is a treatise written in response to a letter directed to Ibn Qutayba according to which the Mutakallimūn accused the people of tradition (*ahl al-ḥadīth*) of lying and expressing contradictory statements so that divisions arose and the Muslim community was split into sects each claiming the truth on the basis of traditions.[6] Ibn Qutayba states that, according to the critics, traditions served opposing groups such as the Khārijites (who considered the grave sinner as an unbeliever) and the Murji'ites (who pointed out that sins do not impair belief), the Qadarites (who held man's free choice) and the Jabrites (who held predestination), the Rāfiḍites (who rejected the *khilāfa* of Abū Bakr and 'Umar) and their adversaries (who preferred both of them to 'Alī), those who prefer wealth and those who prefer poverty (the ascetics, *zuhhād*), the different groups of jurists (*al-fuqahā'*) and the holders of *badā'* (those who believe that God changes His decisions). Believers in anthropomorphic traditions ('God created Adam in His image' or 'the believer's heart is between two of God's fingers') are set forth as examples of those who tell lies concerning God.[7] Moreover, the traditionists relate follies which cause people to disparage Islam, the unbelievers (*al-mulḥidūn*) to laugh at the faith, those who wish to embrace Islam to abstain from it, and which increase the doubts of the sceptics.[8] Ibn Qutayba regards these traditions as forgeries made by the *zanādiqa.*[9] In addition to the contents of traditions which bothered the Mutakallimūn, the traditionists' personalities also annoyed them; they are ignorant and ill-natured.[10]

Now let us investigate the claims against traditions as detailed by

Ibn Qutayba. There are traditions which oppose speculation and rational arguments, such as the Prophet's statement that he is more entitled to be sceptical than Ibrāhīm concerning God's actions.[11] The assumption which lies at the basis of the argument is Muḥammad's perfection, which could not be impaired by doubts. Furthermore, some traditions do not coincide with man's experience. According to a tradition, the Prophet said that no human being would remain on earth in the year AH 100. Now, the opponent maintains that we are in AH 300 and the world is more populated than before.[12]

Most of the examples can be subsumed under the title of contradictory traditions. Such contradictions exist in different domains. It may be in the sphere of leadership; according to one tradition, the leader of the community must be the best person. However, another tradition tells the people that they can pray behind any person whether he be a righteous or a wicked ruler.[13] And in the sphere of jurisprudence, one tradition inflicts cutting off the hand for stealing an egg or a rope, while another states that such a punishment is only for stealing a quarter of a *dīnār*.[14] In the sphere of theology, the relationship between grave sin and belief is also dealt with. There is a contradiction between one tradition which teaches that grave sin does not coincide with belief, while a second tradition states that even a grave sinner will come to Paradise, meaning that he is a believer.[15] Concerning the position of the Prophet, we learn the famous tradition: 'There will be no prophet after me, and no community after my community. The permitted things (*ḥalāl*) are those which God permitted through me [says Muḥammad] until the Resurrection, and the forbidden things are those which God forbade through me until the Resurrection.' Against it stands a tradition no less noteworthy, which reads: 'Jesus Christ will descend [this is one of the signs which precedes the Resurrection], kill the pig, break the cross and increase the number of the permitted things'.[16] Thus Muḥammad is not the last prophet and there will be a change in the number of permitted things.

The rationalists also use the Qur'ān in order to show the illegitimacy of the Tradition. According to Qur'ān 2.180 ('Prescribed for you, when any of you dies, and he leaves behind some goods, is to make testament in favour of his parents and kinsmen ...'), a man must write a testament in favour of his heirs, contrary to a tradition which states that there should not be a testament in favour of an heir (*lā waṣiyata li-wārith*). Ibn Qutayba answers that this verse was abrogated.[17] Also, in the question of *ajal* (the appointed time of death), there is a contradiction between the Qur'ān and the Tradition. Qur'ān 7.34 reads: 'When their *ajal* comes, they shall neither postpone it nor make it come earlier by an hour'. The *ajal* is thus fixed. However, there is a tradition which tells us that man can lengthen his lifetime by doing good for his relatives (*ṣilat al-raḥim tazīdu fi'l-'umr*).[18]

It is not only the Qur'ān which refutes the traditionalists' doctrines, but also the Consensus (*al-ijmā'*). We are told in a tradition that God descends every night to the lowest heaven, which means that in this time He is in a specific place. This contradicts what is known through Qur'ān verses (58.7, 43.84) and through the Consensus that God is everywhere.[19]

In sum, the *ḥadīth*, a very important source of knowledge which, as we have seen, equals, according to some theologians, the Qur'ān, and on which the traditionalists rely, is, according to the rationalists, a device which cannot be relied on, because reason and man's experience contradict its teachings, its nature is self-contradictory, and it is refuted by both the Qur'ān and the Consensus.

In al-Dārimī's *K. al-radd 'alā al-Marīsī*,[20] a different element of criticism is added to the discussion on the absurdities of the *ḥadīth*.[21] This concerns the contention over the sources of traditions. Surprisingly enough, the opponent, who represents al-Marīsī's arguments, cites in the first instance a tradition that states that prophetic traditions will be widely circulated (*sa-yafshū al-ḥadīth 'annī*) and the criterion of their authenticity is their accordance with the Qur'ān (*fa-mā wāfaqa minhā al-qur'ān fa-huwa 'annī wa-mā khālafahu fa-laysa 'annī*).[22] Thus, in the adversary's view, traditionalism itself admits the forgery of some traditions. Al-Dārimī's opponent is not content with this general accusation, and he also adds specific ones. The caliph Mu'āwiyya ibn Abī Sufyān (d. 60/680) is said to have collected unapproved traditions from people and then ascribed them to the Prophet.[23] The same charge is levelled against 'Abdallāh ibn 'Amr ibn al-'Āṣ, who is renowned for transmitting many traditions from Muḥammad. He found during the battle of Yarmūk (15/636) two pack-animals loaded with books of the people of the Book (*ahl al-kitāb*, meaning Jewish and Christian books). He related the contents of these books to his people as traditions traced back to the Prophet. Here, the exact source of the prophetic traditions is indicated.[24] Elsewhere, al-Dārimī set forth the opponent's contention that 12,000 traditions were invented by unbelievers (*zanādiqa*) and put into circulation among negligent transmitters of traditions.[25] The opponent even exploits statements of important traditionists such as Sufyān al-Thawrī (d. 161/778), Shu'ba ibn al-Ḥajjāj (d. 160/776) and 'Abdallāh Ibn al-Mubārak (d. 181/797) to reprove dealing with the *ḥadīth*. For example, Shu'ba says that 'this *ḥadīth* diverts you from the remembrance of God and from prayer ...'.[26]

The Mu'tazilites, who are in many theological issues rationalists, express a subtle attitude towards the *ḥadīth*. Their stand stems from the search for certainty. As an example, I choose to survey 'Abd al-Jabbār's view. Answering their opponents' claim that the Mu'tazila cannot be named *ahl al-sunna wa'l-jamā'a*, since they do not adhere to the Sunna and the Consensus, 'Abd al-Jabbār first defines the Sunna. In his view, Sunna is the Prophet's order which must be carried out perpetually, or his act which must be followed continuously. This definition applies to what is proved as the Prophet's statement or act. Now, a tradition which is based on the authority of a single transmitter (*khabar al-wāḥid*) or single transmitters (*khabar al-āḥād*) and which meets the conditions of trustworthiness is called Sunna according to ordinary usage (*'alā wajh al-ta'āruf*).[27] 'Abd al-Jabbār opposes the consideration of these traditions as true Sunna, because 'we are not safe from being liars concerning this'. Such traditions do not convey certainty, therefore it is forbidden from the point of view of reason to say definitely: 'The Prophet has said it', but one may say: 'It has been related from the Prophet'.[28] Thus, for 'Abd al-Jabbār the majority of traditions are of an uncertain source, due to rational considerations. To defend his attitude towards traditions, he cites statements (mainly of Shu'ba ibn al-Ḥajjāj, whom he names 'Commander of the faithful concerning the Tradition', *amīr al-mu'minīn fī al-ḥadīth*) which espouse the danger of dealing with traditions and the notion that a great many are not genuine. Moreover, he states that if there were no proof of the obligation to carry out acts according to this type of traditions, there would be no benefit in transmitting them. According to the Prophet, the criterion for judging the authenticity of traditions is their agreement with the contents of the Qur'ān and the Sunna, which are known. This criterion is relevant to traditions which deal with practice (*mā trīquhu al-'amal*), but there is no obligation to accept *khabar al-wāḥid*, which deals with theological issues (*mā tarīquhu al-dīn*). 'Abd al-Jabbār censures the traditionists not because of the essence of the Tradition, but rather because of their wrong method and their limited understanding. If reciting the Qur'ān without understanding is detestable in the eyes of the Prophet, the more so with regard to the reading of traditions. In sum, 'Abd al-Jabbār does not oppose *khabar al-āḥād* by virtue of itself, but because many traditions of this kind are spurious and because their transmitters cannot be relied upon due to their negligence and lack of understanding.[29]

We have seen that one of the principles of traditionalism is adherence to and adoration for the teachings of the ancient scholars (*al-salaf*) and for their personalities. From the era in which the criticism against the *salaf* began to flourish, we learn that this principle of traditionalism became firmly rooted in the traditionalists' view beginning with the third/ninth century. The rationalists tried to undermine the firm stand of the *salaf* by discrediting their personalities. The Mu'tazilite al-Naẓẓām refers to the caliph 'Umar ibn al-Khaṭṭāb as being inconsistent in using analogy (*qiyās*) and in his judgements.[30] The same accusations apply to Abū Bakr.[31] The caliph 'Alī does not remain free from blame. 'Alī said: 'Whenever one transmitted to me a tradition of the Prophet (*ḥadaththanī bi-ḥadīth*), I made him swear by God that he had heard it from God's Messenger. If he swore, I believed him.' Al-Naẓẓām reacts to 'Alī's statement, saying: 'The transmitter must be in 'Alī's view either a trustworthy person (*thiqa*) or an untrustworthy one (*muttaham*). Now, if he is trustworthy, making him swear has no meaning, and if he is untrustworthy, how will the saying of the untrustworthy person prove true through his oath? If it is possible for him to transmit false tradition, it is possible for him to swear falsely.'[32] Two conclusions, which attack two principles of traditionalism, can be drawn from this passage: 'Alī's reputation as a wise scholar is impaired, for he established an unreasonable procedure for accepting traditions; and all the traditions in which 'Alī is a transmitter may be suspected as unreliable.

Other members of the *Ṣaḥāba*, who are the bulk of the *salaf*, are also condemned by al-Naẓẓām. 'Abdallāh ibn Mas'ūd (d. 32/652) has uttered contradictory statements. On the one hand he said: 'The permitted thing (*ḥalāl*) is evident (*bayyin*) and the forbidden thing (*ḥarām*) is evident'; but on the other hand he said concerning juridical judgements: 'I speak of them on the basis of my personal judgement (*ra'y*). If I am right, it is from God, and if I am wrong, it is from me.' Consequently, one who follows the juridical judgements of 'Abdallāh ibn Mas'ūd may err and carry out wrong acts, contrary to Ibn Mas'ūd's first statement.[33] 'Abdallāh ibn Mas'ūd is also accused of lying. He claimed, says al-Naẓẓām, that he saw the moon being split (cf. Qur'ān 54.1) for Muḥammad. Al-Naẓẓām responds that this is a lie, for God did not split the moon only for Muḥammad, but He split it as sign for all the people and as proof for the prophecy of Muḥammad.[34] Another criticism of Ibn Mas'ūd is his having been inconsistent and influenced by others in juridical opinions. Al-Naẓẓām relates that Ibn Mas'ūd was asked by the caliph 'Umar about exchange of money and said to the caliph: 'There is no objection to it'. However, after the caliph had said: 'I do not like it', Ibn Mas'ūd said: 'I do not like it, for you do not like it'. Ibn Mas'ud withdrew his first statement without speculation. Al-Naẓẓām says that if this is the behaviour of the best scholar of jurisprudence, what should one think about the behaviour of scholars of lesser rank? How can such scholars be proof against us and how can we obey them?[35]

Al-Naẓẓām cites statements of the *Ṣaḥāba* which show that they admitted that their juridical judgements were made on the basis of assumption (*ẓann*), whereas God has forbidden judgements on the basis of assumption and ordered that judgements should be made in keeping with knowledge and certainty. If this is the case concerning the ancient scholars (*salaf*), the more so concerning those who followed them.[36] In sum, al-Naẓẓām discredits the *salaf* and hence traditionalism.

The *ḥadīth* literature as the sum total of Muḥammad's teaching is discredited by the Zaydite Mutakallim al-Qāsim ibn Ibrāhīm (d. 246/860), who speaks of the possibility that not all the Prophet's sayings were recorded by the *Ṣaḥāba*. He seems to have deduced from this statement that traditions cannot serve as an independent source of information without using the Book.[37]

Al-Naẓẓām is also said to have censured the principle of Consensus (*ijmā'*). As we have seen, the *ijmā'* is legitimised, inter alia, through the *ḥadīth*: 'My community does not agree on an error' (*lā tajtami'u ummatī 'alā ḍalāla*).[38] Contrary to this tradition, al-Naẓẓām states that it is possible for Muslims to agree on an error (*khaṭa'*).[39] In *K. al-nakth* (p. 115), there is a different version of al-Naẓẓām's statement according to which the community may agree on a subjective error (*ḍalāla*), meaning an error based on personal opinion (*ra'y*) or analogy (*qiyās*), but not on an objective fault (*khaṭa'*), which derives from transmission of knowledge through the senses. Al-Khayyāṭ (*K. al-intiṣār*, p. 44) denies the ascription of this statement to al-Naẓẓām, saying that it is known only through the medium of al-Jāḥiẓ. Al-Naẓẓām also states that the community agreed that only Muḥammad had been sent to all the people on earth, whereas the truth is that every prophet was sent to all the people, for God's miracles reach every place on earth.[40] According to him, the *ijmāʿ* of the *Ṣaḥāba* was wrong on account of their contradictory statements in matters of law.[41] ʿAbd al-Jabbār, who accepts the Consensus as proof (*al-Mughnī*, vol. 17, pp. 160ff.), states that the Consensus is not necessarily the consensus of the majority. In his view, the *jamāʿa*, a term which is equal, as we have seen, to the *ijmāʿ*, is the agreement with (*mujāmaʿa*) the people of truth (*ahl al-ḥaqq*) even if they are few. He accepts the notion of al-Naẓẓām that many people may err, and cites Qur'ān verses, such as 11.40, 'Only a few people believed with him (Nūḥ),' which praise the few.[42] Other verses are cited to show that the Qur'ān recommends asking and obeying the wise people and not the *jamāʿa*. 'Ask the people of remembrance if you do not know' (Qur'ān 21.7) and 'Obey God and obey the Messenger and those who are wise, (literally 'those in authority', *ūlū al-amr*).[43] Also, the beginning of Muḥammad's career proves that the truth may be with the few, Muḥammad and his first followers, and not with the many, the pagans in Makka. The experiences of other prophets prove the same notion.[44]

The criticism of rituals and commandments which occupies a central place in the works of heretics such as Ibn al-Rāwandī (see notes 1 and 4 above) is almost absent from the writings of the rationalists. I found only a few examples in Ibn Qutayba's treatise. He relates that the Baghdadi Muʿtazilite Thumāma ibn Ashras (d. 213/828), when seeing people run on Friday to the mosque for fear of missing the prayer,[45] said: 'Look at the cattle, look at the donkeys ... What this Arabian [meaning the Prophet] has done to the people.'[46] According to Ibn Qutayba, the Mutakallimūn even regard some of God's prohibitions as essentially unbinding. For example, wine is not forbidden in itself, but only for the purpose of education.[47] Other Mutakallimun, says Ibn Qutayba, consider the fat and the skin of swine permitted for use, for God only forbade the flesh of swine (Qur'ān 5.3 'Forbidden to you are carrion, blood, the flesh of swine ...'[48]). Here, the literal meaning of a verse serves as a weapon of libertinism against traditionalism. However, this criticism remained marginal; the main target of the rationalists' attacks was the *ḥadīth* and its transmitters.

6

COMPROMISE BETWEEN RATIONALISM AND TRADITIONALISM

In Islamic theology, the compromise between rationalism and traditionalism (using both terms as defined in the introduction) can be shown on the basis of two versions. In the first, reason and Tradition constitute separate tools, each responsible for the knowledge of certain religious principles. Here there is no contradiction between reason and revelation, for either these devices do not meet in one and the same issue, or if they do, they teach from two points of view. Al-Bāqillānī and Abū al-Ḥusayn al-Baṣrī speak of issues which can be known through the intellect and others through Tradition.[1] Using both methods is legitimate from the point of view of religion. It is also possible that a theologian would use both Tradition and reason concerning the same issue, either to prove its existence or to prove a certain aspect of it. According to al-Ghazālī, Tradition and reason appear in the treatment of the Resurrection, the first as a means of knowing its reality and truth and the second being what is incumbent on man. 'Resurrection is mentioned by Revelation, it is true (or: it is really exists) and one must believe in it, for it is possible according to the intellect.'[2] However, it should be noted that al-Ghazālī's attitude towards reason and Tradition is not homogeneous. Sometimes he distinguishes between reason in general and speculative theology (*kalām*) in particular. Whereas reason, or philosophical reasoning, occupies an important place in his theology and in certain issues the paramount place,[3] the systems of the Kalām do not receive similar treatment; on the contrary, in *Iḥyā'* the aim of the Kalām is to safeguard the belief of the common people (*al-'awāmm*) from the confusion introduced by the innovators. The common people are easily aroused by the disputation (*jadal*) of the innovators, even if it is false. And to reject this false disputation one must use a false device, meaning the Kalām. Speculative arguments should be considered a dangerous medicine; it must be given in the place in which it is needed, in the appropriate time, and in a measure according to necessity.[4] However, in his *al-Mustaṣfā*, the Kalām is the highest science.[5] There is a difference between al-Ghazālī's early work *al-Iqtiṣād* and his later works, *al-Mustaṣfā* and *al-Qisṭās*. In the early work, what the intellect regards as inconceivable, for example anthropomorphic expressions, should be interpreted figuratively,[6] for it is inadmissible that Revelation should contain texts which contradict reason.[7] Thus al-Ghazālī raises reason above Tradition, a stand which he shares with Ibn Rushd. Although al-Ghazālī condemns the Kalām, he states that if the intellect is used in an appropriate manner, which means not as used by some Mutakallimūn, man can obtain the truth concerning metaphysical issues. And this truth is consistent with what can be found in revelation.[8] As we have seen,[9] al-Ghazālī also holds that rational arguments are an integral part of Revelation, and hence he concludes that there can be no contradiction between reason and Revelation. This conclusion was later drawn by Ibn Taymiyya in his *Dar' ta'āruḍ al-'aql wa'l-naql*.

The second form of compromise between reason and Tradition, the notion that rational arguments do not contradict traditional ones, was already advanced by the Zaydite imam al-Hādī ilā al-Ḥaqq Yaḥyā ibn al-Ḥusayn ibn al-Qāsim ibn Ibrāhīm (d. 298/910) in his *al-Radd 'alā ahl al-zaygh min al-mushabbihīn*. In Yaḥyā's view, which was very probably based on the teaching of the Mu'tazila, arguments, be they rational or traditional, cannot contradict each other, for they are God's. God provides man with two kinds of revelations, the Qur'ān and the proofs of the intellect, therefore there can be no contradiction between reason and Tradition. Moreover, the intellect proves what the Qur'ān and the Sunna affirm, and vice versa. The rejection of anthropomorphism is adduced as an example of the absence of contradiction between reason and Revelation. Qur'ān 42.11 and 112.1–4 are brought as proof that God is unlike anything. Likewise, the intellect affirms the unlikeness of God to the creation.[10] It must be emphasised that this notion must be differentiated from the notion according to which the Messenger urges the people to deliberate. In the latter, the intellect is not a form of revelation but man's predisposition for using rational arguments to attain truth. The function of the prophet is to activate this ability. In his commentary to Qur'ān 17.15, 'We never chastise, until We send forth a Messenger' (tr. Arberry), the Mu'tazilite exegete al-Zamakhsharī (538/1143) states that if God did not send forth messengers to the people, the latter could say that they were inattentive.[11] Ibn Taymiyya adopts a notion which in certain aspects resembles that of the Muʿtazila, and he may have been influenced by their teachings. Like the Muʿtazila, he considers the proofs of the intellect to be God's, but whereas in the Muʿtazila the rational proofs are produced in man, in Ibn Taymiyya the rational proofs are an integral part of the Qur'ān.

> The Qur'ān's indication (*dalāla*)[12] of things is divided into two kinds: (1) God's trustworthy message ... and (2) the Qur'ān's parables and its explanation of rational proofs which indicate what is sought for. This last indication is both revelational and rational (*dalāla sharʿiyya ʿaqliyya*). It is revelational, because the Qur'ān (or revelation, *al-sharʿ*) indicates it and guides man to it, and it is rational, because its veracity is known through the intellect.[13]

Moreover, in many places he states that what man obtains through pure intellect is consistent with what the Messenger affirmed. The information gained through man's pure intellect does not contradict the information gained through pure tradition (*laysa bayna al-maʿqūl al-ṣarīḥ wa'l-manqūl al-ṣarīḥ tanāquḍ aṣlan*).[14] This statement proves that Ibn Taymiyya thinks that apart from the rational arguments located in the Revelation, there are arguments which man gains by means of his intellectual efforts. If these arguments are built in an appropriate way, they do not contradict the contents of the Revelation. Contradiction between the Revelation and reason occurs only when either the intellect produces false arguments, or a tradition is weak or apocryphal.[15] It seems to me, contrary to what I have stated elsewhere,[16] that in addition to Qur'ānic arguments, there are arguments which man produces. Thus Ibn Taymiyya also maintains the independent status of rational proofs.

Apart from general systems of harmonisation of reason and Tradition, there have also been efforts aimed at specific theological issues. Thus the theory of *kasb* may be viewed as an attempt at harmonising the rational requisite of free will and the traditional dogma of predestination.[17]

7
SUMMARY

The following are the main conclusions arrived at in this book. The basic difference between Muslim traditionalists and rationalists is the latter's use of rational proofs as a source of religious knowledge and as a point of departure to attack the traditionalists. As we have seen, pure rationalism is absent from Islamic theology, and the denomination 'rationalist' applies to those who use rational proofs as their primary source for producing certain theological theses. This enables us to differentiate between degrees of rationalism which are established according to the measure of rational proofs used. The Muʿtazilites are thus best entitled to this name, whereas other Mutakallimūn such as Ashʿarites or Māturīdites occupy the second place in such a theoretical hierarchy. The rationalists have been more inclined than the traditionalists to employ rational arguments to support theological tenets which derive from Tradition. Whereas pure rationalism is absent from Islamic theology, there is pure (or extreme) traditionalism, although this phenomenon has been limited to a small number of scholars. By a pure traditionalist we mean a theologian who does not use rational proofs at all, neither as a source of religious knowledge nor as corroboration for doctrines derived from the *samʿ*, namely, the Qur'ān, the Sunna and the Consensus, nor as a weapon against his adversaries. The second type of traditionalist is one who bases his doctrines on *samʿ*, but uses rational arguments either to support his doctrines or to refute his adversaries (for example Ibn Ḥanbal). Among the traditionalists, extremism is not the privilege of the Ḥanbalites alone, but can be found in scholars of other schools. There is diffusion of ideas in all the schools of law and theology; a theologian is not always committed to the teachings of his school. Thus scholars, such as Ibn Taymiyya, who introduce themselves as bitter opponents of Kalām, nevertheless use the systems of the Kalām. Rational solutions to theological problems, such as the use of figurative speech as a remedy for anthropomorphism, penetrate circles of Mutakallimūn who are known as followers of Ash'arisim. Usually the Ash'arites apply the theory of *bi-lā kayfa*, and this last theory appears in a Mu'tazilite scholar. As we have seen in Fakhr al-Dīn al-Rāzī's theory of prophethood, a scholar may be a traditionalist then a rationalist.

The foundations of traditionalism and rationalism stand in sharp contrast. At one end of the spectrum are the internal roots of Islam – the Qur'ān, the Sunna and the Consensus, all of which produce homogeneous doctrines (however, this statement is not always right), and the ancient scholars and their true and legitimate doctrines. And at the other end of the spectrum is an external device – reason (though not always considered as an external device; sometimes it constitutes a kind of revelation and sometimes it is included in revelation), which produces various solutions to theological issues and at times defames the ancient scholars on account of rational considerations. Each trend reacts to the foundations and to the doctrines which are drawn from the opposing trend; and the more extreme the rationalist is, the more offensive he is to the traditionalists and vice versa. The traditionalists use reason in order to refute the rationalists, while the rationalists do not refrain from using Qur'ānic interpretation and traditions to refute the traditionalists. Sometimes rationalists and traditionalists use similar arguments which derive from different premises, such as the argument that reason or Tradition leads to contradictory tenets. The battlefield is not always clear, for the traditionalists sometimes wear the clothes of the rationalists.[1] Therefore, it is better to speak of rationalist tendencies than to speak of rationalism.

APPENDIX I

THE CREED OF ABŪ ZUR'A 'UBAYDALLĀH IBN 'ABD AL-KARĪM AL-RĀZĪ (D. 264/878) AND ABŪ ḤĀTIM MUḤAMMAD IBN IDRĪS AL-RĀZĪ (D. 277/890)[1]

(p. 176)

1. Belief is action and saying (*qawl wa-'amal*), it increases and decreases (*yazīdu wa-yanquṣu*).[2]
2. The Qur'ān is God's uncreated speech (*kalām Allāh ghayr makhlūq*) in all its aspects.[3]
3. Predestination (*qadar*), whether good or evil, derives from God.[4]
4. The best persons of this community after its Prophet are Abū Bakr al-Ṣiddīq, then 'Umar ibn al-Khaṭṭāb, then 'Uthmān ibn 'Affān, then 'Alī. (p. 177) They are the rightly guided caliphs.[5]
5. There are ten persons whom God's Messenger called the people of Paradise and testified that they would be there. It is his true statement. One must have mercy upon all Muḥammad's Companions and abstain from [dealing with controversies] which took place among them.[6]
6. God is on His Throne (*'arshihi*) and is separated from His creation as He described Himself in His Book and through His Messenger 'without modality' (*bi-lā kayfa*).[7] God knows everything thoroughly: 'There is none like Him and He is the All-Hearing and the All-Seeing' (Qur'ān 42.11).
7. God will be seen in the world to come.[8] The people of Paradise will see Him with their eyes (literally 'glances') and will hear His speech in the manner He wills and as He wills.
8. Both Paradise and Hell really exist. Both of them are created entities which will never perish.[9] Paradise is reward for God's friends (*awliyā'ihi*) and Hell is punishment for sinners (literally 'those who disobey God', *ahl ma'ṣiyatihi*), unless God will have mercy upon them.[10]
9. The Way (*al-ṣirāṭ*) is true.[11]
10. The Balance (*al-mīzān*) is true. It has two scales in which man's good and evil deeds are weighed. [All this is] true.[12]

11. The Basin (*al-ḥawḍ*), through which our Prophet is honoured, is true.[13]
12. The Intercession (*al-shafāʿa*) is true.[14]
13. The Resurrection (*al-baʿth*) after death is true.[15]
14. People who commit grave sins are subject to God's will.[16]
15. We do not declare the Muslims (literally 'the people who direct their prayer toward the Kaʿba', *ahl al-qibla*) to be unbelievers on account of their sins, and we entrust their secrets to God.[17]
16. We carry out the precepts of the Holy War (*jihād*) and Pilgrimage (*ḥajj*) with the leaders of the Muslims in every period.[18]
17. We do not consider rebellion against the leaders of the community and strife in civil war appropriate. We listen to and obey those whom God appoints as our leaders and we shall not stop obeying [them]. We follow the Sunna and the Consensus (*jamāʿa*) and abstain from deviations (*shudhūdh*), controversy (*khilāf*) and disunion (*furqa*).[19]

(p. 178)

18. The Holy War continues from the time of Muḥammad until the Resurrection with the powerful leaders of the Muslims, nothing will cancel it.
19. Likewise the Pilgrimage and giving obligatory offerings in the form of cattle to powerful leaders of the Muslims [continue].
20. People must be treated as believers (literally 'people are believers') in accordance with the rules of believers and their inheritance. We do not know what they are in the eyes of God.[20]
21. Whoever says that he is truly a believer is an innovator. Whoever says that he is a believer in the eyes of God is a liar.[21] And whoever says that he is truly a believer in God is right.
22. The Murji'ites and the innovators are deviators (*ḍulāl*).
23. The innovative Qadarites are deviators. Whoever, among them, denies that God knows what happens before it happens is an unbeliever.[22]
24. The Jahmites are unbelievers.[23]
25. The Rāfidites rejected (*rafaḍū*) Islām.[24]
26. The Khārijites are apostates (*murāq*).[25]
27. Whoever claims that the Qur'ān was created (*makhlūq*) does not believe in the Mighty God. His unbelief removes him from the community. Whoever doubts his unbelief, among those who understand, is an unbeliever.
28. Whoever has doubts concerning God's speech hesitating and

saying: I do not know whether it was created or not, is a Jahmite.[26]

29. Whoever hesitates concerning the Qur'ān without knowing is an innovator and not an unbeliever.[27]

(p. 179)

30. Whoever says: My uttering of the Qur'ān is created, or the Qur'ān in my uttering is created is a Jahmite.
31. Abū Muḥammad ('Abd al-Raḥmān ibn Abū Ḥātim) said: I heard my father saying: The sign of the innovators (*ahl al-bida'*) is their defaming of the traditionists (*ahl al-athar*), and the sign of the heretics (*zanādiqa*) is their naming *ahl al-sunna* as *ḥashwiyya* wishing through this the cancellation of traditions. The sign of the Jahmites is their naming of *ahl al-sunna* as likeners (*mushabbiha*). The sign of the Qadarites is their naming of the traditionists as *mujbira* (those who adhere to predestination). The sign of the Murji'ites is their naming of *ahl al-sunna* as opposers (*mukhālifa*) and as *nuqṣāniyya* (those who state that belief increases and decreases [*naqaṣa*]). The sign of the Rāfiḍites is their naming of *ahl al-sunna* as *nāṣiba.*

    Only one name is attached to *ahl al-sunna*, and it is impossible that all these names should apply to them.

I would like to point out some other dogmas which I have found in the creeds of other scholars mentioned by al-Lālakā'ī and which are not set out in the present creed. Despite al-Lālakā'ī's statement on the homogeneity of the teachings of *ahl al-sunna wa'l-jamā'a* (see Chapter 1, n. 50), the following list proves that even among the traditionalists there was no general consensus concerning articles of faith. I do not mean to say that a scholar who did not introduce one of the following articles did not believe in it, but the absence of a certain article shows at least that he did not ascribe importance to it. Out of the ten creeds which occur in al-Lālakā'ī, eight seem to be complete creeds. These are the creeds of Sufyān al-Thawrī, Sufyān ibn 'Uyayna, Ibn Ḥanbal, 'Alī ibn al-Madīnī, al-Bukhārī, Sahl al-Tustarī, Ibn Jarīr al-Ṭabarī, and Abū Ḥātim and Abū Zur'a. What appears as the *i'tiqād* of al-Awzā'ī and of Abū Thawr al-Kalbī is no more than several statements on belief.

1. Wiping off the shoes (*al-masḥ 'alā al-khufayn*).[28]
2. Lowering of the voice when uttering the formula 'In the name of God, the Merciful, the Compassionate' (*bi-smi allāh al-raḥmān al-raḥīm*) in the prayer.[29]

3. Following the ancient scholars (*al-salaf*).[30]
4. Belief in and acceptance of traditions as they are without questions of 'why' and 'how'.[31]
5. The Punishment of the Tomb (*'adhāb al-qabr*).[32]
6. The Prophet saw God.[33]
7. The Antichrist will appear and Jesus will kill him.[34]
8. Whoever does not pray is unbeliever, and God permits his killing.[35]
9. Whoever commits a sin, for which there is the punishment of Hell, and then repents, God will forgive him.[36]
10. The adulterer must be stoned.[37]
11. There are traditions which must not be interpreted.[38]
12. Discussion of predestination and other issues of the Sunna is reprehensible (*al-kalām fī al-qadar wa-ghayrihi min al-sunna makrūh*).[39]
13. Whoever defames or hates one of the Companions is an innovator.[40]
14. Hypocrisy (*nifāq*) amounts to unbelief (*kufr*).[41]
15. It is forbidden to fight against this community.[42]
16. One has to forsake the Mutakallimūn's views and their company and the company of whoever composes books according to personal opinions and not according to traditions.[43]
17. The discussion of what 'name' (*ism*) and what 'the object named' (*al-musammā*) are is stupidity.[44]

APPENDIX II

AL-MUKHTAṢAR FĪ UṢŪL AL-DĪN[1]

(p. 197)

Q: What must the person obliged know concerning the principles of religion (*uṣūl al-dīn*)?[2]

A: He must know four issues: (1) God's unity (*tawḥīd*);[3] (2) God's justice (*ʿadl*);[4] (3) Prophecies (*nubuwwāt*); and (4) Laws (*sharāʾiʿ*).

(p. 199)

Q: What is the first obligation incumbent on man?

A: It is speculation and reflection which leads to the knowledge of God.

Q: First, what is the source of our knowledge that speculation and reflection are obligatory, whereas some people, such as the traditionists (*ahl al-ḥadīth*), oppose this notion and state that knowledge is gained through uncritical acceptance of ideas (*al-ʿilm bi'l-taqlīd*)?[5] Moreover, some learned people state that knowledge is obtained necessarily and there is no need to reflect and speculate.

A: The learned man knows that there are people who are wrong in their speculation (*yukhṭiʾu*) and others who are right (*yuṣību*), however each of them claims that he is right. Why, then, is the *taqlīd* of one of them better than the *taqlīd* of the other? Why is the *taqlīd* of the believer in God's unity better than the *taqlīd* of the unbeliever? Why is the *taqlīd* of whoever believes in the seeing of God better than the *taqlīd* of whoever denies this seeing?

(p. 200)

This explains the incorrectness of the *taqlīd* and proves that the truth cannot be known through people …

The proof that the knowledge of God and His Messenger can be obtained through reflection is that if it were obtained through necessary knowledge the learned people would hold the same notions and would not differ concerning them ... What proves our idea, from the point of view of tradition (*al-samʿ*), is that God enjoins speculation and urges people to it; He praises those who speculate and denounces those who deviate from it and says: 'Speculate about what is in the heavens and in the earth' (Qur'ān 10.101) and 'Do they not speculate about how the camels were created?' (Qur'ān 88.17) and '[In the earth there are signs ...] and in yourselves, do you not see'? (Qur'ān 51.21) and 'How many a sign there is in the heavens and in the earth that they pass by, turning away from it' (Qur'ān 12.105). The Qur'ānic arguments to which God calls man's attention prove the obligation to speculate and the incorrectness of the *taqlīd*.[6]

(p. 201)

Q: What is the proof that the learned man must speculate in order to obtain the knowledge of God?

A: That is because if he hears the people's controversies concerning these systems of thought, the charge of unbelief through which they accuse each other (*takfīr*) and each of them frightening his colleague as a result of the controversy, and if he knows that it is impossible that all these systems of thought should be right, for each contradicts the other, for example the notion that the world is eternal vis-à-vis the notion that the world was created, the notion that God can be seen vis-à-vis the notion that He cannot be seen, and [if he knows] that it is also impossible that all these systems can be wrong, for the truth lies within one of them, that is, it is inconceivable that the world should not be eternal and should not have been created, [he will necessarily know that] there are systems which are right and others which are wrong.

APPENDIX III

TWO PASSAGES ON REASON AND TRADITION

A CHAPTER WHICH DETAILS WHAT CAN BE KNOWN THROUGH REASON AND NOT THROUGH TRADITION, WHAT CAN BE KNOWN ONLY THROUGH TRADITION AND NOT THROUGH REASON AND WHAT CAN BE KNOWN THROUGH BOTH REASON AND TRADITION[1]

(p. 228)

Know, may God have mercy upon you, that all the known principles of religion (*aḥkām*[2] *al-dīn al-ma'lūma*) must be divided into three kinds: (1) what may be known only through reason (*al-'aql*) and not through Tradition (or Revelation – *al-sam'*); (2) what may not be known through reason, but may be known only through Tradition; and (3) what may be known both through reason and Tradition.

As for what may be known only through reason and not through Tradition, these are the creation of the world (*ḥudūth al-'ālam*), the proof of the existence of its creator (*muḥdith*),[3] His being one (*waḥdāniyatihi*), His attributes, the prophecy of His messengers and all that which is connected to these matters, namely, the knowledge of God's unity and prophecy which may only be obtained through reason.

The proof of this is that Tradition (*al-sam'*) is only God's speech (*kalām allāh*, meaning the Qur'ān) and the statements (*qawl*, meaning the *ḥadīth*) of him who is known as God's Messenger and the Consensus (*ijmā'*) of those who are reported not to have erred in their opinions. It is impossible to know that the speech is God's, that the statements are His Messenger's and the trustworthiness and rightness of those whom the Messenger declared to be trustworthy and right, unless one knows God's existence beforehand. That is because the knowledge that the speech is God's and that the Messenger is His Messenger constitutes a branch of the knowledge of God's existence, for God is known through His speech, His sending (of messengers) and His attributes. And it is impossible for one to know God's attributes, unless one knows God's existence, just as it is impossible for one who does not know Zayd's existence to know his speech and his messenger. Therefore, the knowledge of God and of the prophecy of His messengers must be known through reason before the knowledge of the rightness of tradition.[4]

(p. 231)

As for what is known through Tradition – things in which reason plays no role – it is the knowledge that the actions of the person obliged (*fi'l al-mukallaf*) are either good or evil, permitted or forbidden ... obligatory or recommended ...[5]

As for what may be known sometimes through reason and sometimes through Tradition, these include all rules or rational issues, the ignorance of which does not infringe the knowledge of God's unity and prophecy, for example the knowledge of the possibility of seeing God, the knowledge of the possibility of forgiveness for the sinner, the knowledge that it is appropriate to act according to tradition based on one transmitter (*khabar al-wāḥid*), the knowledge of using analogy in laws, and so on. If the person obliged does not know such issues, his ignorance does not prevent him from knowing God and the prophecy of His messengers.[6]

A CHAPTER ON WHAT IS KNOWN THROUGH RATIONAL PROOFS AND WHAT IS KNOWN THROUGH TRADITIONAL PROOFS[7]

Know that things known through proof can be possibly known either through reason (*'aql*) alone, or through Tradition (*shar'*) alone, or through both Tradition and reason. The things known through reason alone are those for which there is a rational proof and the knowledge of the soundness of Tradition is based on the knowledge of it (this rational proof), such as the knowledge of God('s existence) and His attributes and that He is All-sufficient and does not do evil. We say: 'The knowledge of the soundness of Tradition is based on the knowledge of rational proof', for we know the soundness of Tradition only if we know the trustworthiness of the prophets, and we know their trustworthiness through miracles only if we know that it is impossible for God to show miracles by the medium of a liar. And this last knowledge is obtained only if we know that showing miracles through a liar is evil and God does not do evil. We know that God does not do evil only if we know that He knows the evilness of evil and does not need the evil things. This knowledge is a branch of the knowledge of God. Therefore these pieces of knowledge must precede the knowledge of Tradition.

As for what it is possible to know through both Tradition and reason, these are all the things for which there are rational proofs and the knowledge of the soundness of Tradition is not based on the knowledge of these proofs, such as the knowledge that God is one and that there is no other god whose wisdom equals that of God. That is because if His wisdom is proved, and if there were another as wise as He, it would be inconceivable for both of them, or one of them, to send one who would lie.[8] Therefore, if the messenger informs that God is one and that there is no other eternal entity with Him, we will know his trustworthiness. Likewise, the obligation to return deposit (*wujūb radd al-wadīʿa*) and the benefit which is gained without damaging anyone (are known through both tradition and reason).

As for what is known through Tradition (*al-sharʿ*) alone, it is that for which Tradition (*al-samʿ*), and not reason, has proof such as traditional benefits and damages (*al-maṣāliḥ wa'l-mafāsid al-sharʿiyya*) and what is connected with them. The traditional benefits and damages are the actions through which Tradition calls upon us to worship God either through carrying out or omitting these actions, such as the obligation to pray and the prohibition against drinking wine and the like.

APPENDIX IV

KITĀB UṢŪL AL-ʿADL WA'L-TAWḤĪD WA-NAFY AL-JABR WA'L-TASHBĪH[1]

(p. 124)

The worship of God is divided into three parts: (1) knowledge of God; (2) knowledge of what pleases Him and what displeases Him; and (3) practising what pleases Him and abstaining from what displeases Him ...

These three kinds of worship derive from three proofs which God introduces to man: reason (*ʿaql*), the Qur'ān and the Messenger.

The proof of reason produces the knowledge of God, the proof of the Book produces the knowledge of worship (*al-taʿabbud*) and the proof of the Messenger produces the knowledge of the practical ways of worship (*ʿibāda*). Reason is the basis of the Qur'ān and the Messenger, (p. 125) for they both are known through reason, whereas reason is not known through them.

The Consensus (*ijmāʿ*) is the fourth proof which includes all three proofs and derives from them.[2]

Know that each of these proofs has a root (*aṣl*) and a branch. The branch must be returned to the root, for the roots judge the branches.

The root of reason is what the learned people agree on and do not differ on, and its branch is what they differ on and do not agree on ...

The root of the Qur'ān is the self-evident (*muḥkam*) [part of it] on which there is an agreement and whose interpretation (*ta'wīl*) does not contradict its plain meaning (*tanzīl*).[3] The branch of the Qur'ān is the ambiguous (*mutashābih*) [part of it] which must be returned to its root on which there is no disagreement among the interpreters (*ahl al-ta'wīl*).[4]

The root of the Sunna of the Prophet is what Muslims agree on, and its branch is what they differ on concerning what came from the Prophet. Every tradition on which there is disagreement must be returned to the roots of reason, the Book and the Consensus.

(p. 126)

The knowledge of God is rational. It is divided into two aspects: affirmation and negation. Affirmation means certain knowledge of God (al-*yaqīn bi-allāh*) and acknowledgment of Him, and negation means negation of His anthropomorphism (*tashbīh*), which in turn is a declaration of His unity (*tawḥīd*).

NOTES

INTRODUCTION

1. Arberry, *Revelation and Reason*, p. 9.
2. Cicero, *De Natura Deorum*, III.
3. *Al-Fārābī on the Perfect State. Abū Naṣr al-Fārābī's Mabādi' Arā' Ahl al-Madīna al-Fāḍila*, ed. trans. and comm. R. Walzer, Oxford 1985, pp. 474–81. D. Gutas, *Avicenna and the Aristotelian Tradition, Introduction to Reading Avicenna's Philosophical Works*, Leiden 1988, pp. 299–307. Ibn Rushd tries a kind of compromise between religion and revelation, according to which since the Qur'ān itself urges people to speculate in order to attain the truth, there can be no contradiction between the demonstrative inquiry and revelation; both of them are true devices. *Faṣl al-maqāl wa-taqrīr mā bayna al-sharī'a wa'l ḥikma min al-ittiṣāl*, ed. G. F. Hourani, Leiden 1959, p. 5f. Ed. Muḥammad 'Imāra, p. 31f.
4. Tr. by S. van den Bergh, London 1954. This work includes the translation of both al-Ghazālī's *Tahāfut al-falāsifa* and Ibn Rushd's *Tahāfut al-tahāfut*.
5. The Zaydite theologian al-Qāsim ibn Ibrāhīm (d. 246/860), who was prone to Mu'tazilism, wrote a treatise against a philosopher or a sceptic entitled *K. al-radd 'alā al-mulḥid*, MS Berlin (W. Ahlwardt, *Verzeichnis der arabischen Handschriften der Königlichen Bibliothek zu Berlin*, Berlin 1887–9, vol. 4, p. 290, no. 4876, Glaser 101), fols 58b–63b, ed. Muḥammad Yaḥyā 'Azzān, Ṣan'ā' 1992. In this epistle, the main issue is the refutation of the eternity of the world. In his *al-Mabāḥith al-Mashriqiyya*, Fakhr al-Dīn al-Rāzī sometimes criticises Ibn Sīnā's views but also accepts some notions of the philosopher. Ibn Taymiyya seems to have been the most prolific theologian in refuting philosophy. See, for example, *Kitāb bughyat al-murtād fī'l-radd 'alā al-mutafalsifa wa'l-qarāmiṭa wa'l-bāṭiniyya*, Cairo AH 1329. In his *Naqḍ al-manṭiq* (p. 44), Ibn Taymiyya points out that the Ash'arite theologian al-Bāqillānī (d. 404/1013) wrote a work entitled *K. al-daqā'iq* in which he refuted the views of the philosophers concerning the spheres, the stars, the intellects, the souls, logic and so on. Al-Suyūṭī's refutation of the Aristotelian logic (*Jahd al-qarīḥa fī tajrīd al-naṣīḥa* [The Exertion of Effort in Divesting the *Naṣīḥa*], which constitutes the second volume of his *Ṣawn*) is an abridgement of Ibn Taymiyya's *Naṣīḥat ahl al-īmān fī al-radd 'alā manṭiq al-yūnān* (the alternative title is *al-Radd 'alā al-manṭiqiyyīn* – The

Refutation of the Logicians). For a discussion and translation of *Jahd al-qarīḥa*, see W. B. Hallaq, *Ibn Taymiyya Against the Greek Logicians*, Oxford 1993. Several Muslim theologians before Ibn Taymiyya have criticised the Aristotelian logic. Ibid. pp. 42–7. For passages of refutation of philosophical views in theological works, see for example Ibn al-Jawzī, *Talbīs Iblīs*, pp. 45–50. Ibn Ḥazm, *al-Fiṣal*, vol. 1, pp. 9–14.

6. Kraemer, *Humanism*, p. 181.
7. In his *Revelation and Reason in Islam*, Arberry devotes most of his work to philosophy, and the scanty discussion of theological issues is not satisfactory. The state of research in this field is best exemplified through the absence of any study which examines the doctrine of *bi-lā kayfa*, one of the most important doctrines of the traditionalists. For discussion of this issue, see my 'The *bi-lā kayfa* Doctrine and its Foundations in Islamic Theology', *Arabica* 42:3 (1995), pp. 365–79. Tritton's article ('Reason and Revelation', *Arabic and Islamic Studies in Honor of Hamilton A. R. Gibb*, ed. G. Makdisi, Leiden 1965, pp. 619–30) deals briefly with speculative theologians and philosophers but ignores the theology of the traditionalists.
8. An excellent example of such a phenomenon is a treatise entitled *Qatf al-thamar fī bayān ʿaqīdat ahl al-athar* ('Picking the fruits concerning the explanation of the creed of the people of Tradition') written by an Indian Muslim scholar Muḥammad Ṣiddīq Ḥasan Khān al-Qinnawjī (d. 1307/1889) and edited by ʿĀṣim ibn Abdallah al-Qaryūṭī, Beirut 1984. Apart from al-Qinnawjī's adherence to the Qur'ān, the Sunna and the views of the Ṣaḥāba and the Tābiʿūn (ibid., p. 42), he states that one should keep away from the innovators (*ahl al-bidaʿ*) and abstain from controversy in religious matters. As examples of innovators, he points out the ancient sects, the Rāfiḍites, the Khārijites, the Jahmites and so on without applying to them modern meanings.
9. It is to be noted that the third/ninth century is established as a point of departure, for in this era the notion of traditionalism has begun to be crystallised. In the second/eighth century, Muḥammad's Tradition has not yet occupied its central position regarding practice and creed. Most of the texts studied belong to the period between the third/ninth and the eighth/fourteenth centuries.
10. *fī anna ahl al-sunna lā yukaffirūna musliman bi-dhanbin wa-bidʿatin wa-lā yamnaʿūna al-ṣalāta khalfahu. Rasāʾil wa-fatāwā shaykh al-islām fī'l-tafsīr wa'l-ḥadīth wa'l-uṣūl wa'l-ʿaqāʾid wa'l-ādāb wa'l-aḥkām*, ed. Muḥammad Rashīd Riḍā, Cairo 1992 (repr.), vol. 2, part 5, p. 241.
11. 'Ḥanbalite Islam', p. 240. Cf. Reinhart, *Before Revelation*, pp. 24, 27, 34, 195, n. 13 (quoting Makdisi, 'Ḥanbalite Islam', p. 239). Ibn Taymiyya himself tried to protect the Ḥanbalites from their reputation as the only extremists in religion. Referring to the issue of the affirmation of God's attributes or their negation, Ibn Taymiyya states that 'the affirmation of attributes does not particularise the Ḥanbalites, and extremism (*ghuluww*) [in this issue] which occurs in them occurs also in others. Moreover, whoever investigates the people's systems will find in each group extremists (*ghulāt*) concerning negation and affirmation which he will not find in the Ḥanbalites.' *Naqḍ al-manṭiq*, p. 139. From Abū al-Ḥasan Muḥammad ibn ʿAbd al-Malik al-Karjī's (d. 532/

1137) condemnation of those who adhere to a certain school in matters of law (e.g. Ḥanbalism) and to another school in matters of theology (e.g. Mu'tazilism), we learn that the boundaries which mark out the schools were not closed. Ibid., p. 144 (quoting al-Karjī's *al-Fuṣūl fī 'l-uṣūl 'an al-a'imma al-fuḥūl*). It is also impossible to state that a certain school of law has always been committed to a certain theological school. Baghdad of the fourth/tenth century attests to leading Ḥanafite scholars who were Mu'tazilites and other Ḥanafites who opposed Mu'tazilism. Madelung, 'The Spread of Māturīdism', p. 112.

12. *The Encyclopedia of Religion*, ed. M. Eliade, New York and London 1987, vol. 15, p. 1.
13. For the distinction between *ḥadīth* and *sunna*, see I. Goldziher, *Muslim Studies*, vol. 2, ch. 1, pp. 24–5.
14. Other appellations which are not in common use are: *ahl al-kitāb wa'l-sunna, ahl al-ḥaqq wa'l-sunna, ahl al-ḥaqq*. Ibn Baṭṭa, *Sharḥ*, p. 11, n. 1. The term which combines the Qur'ān, the Sunna and the Consensus is *al-sam'* (literally 'hearing'). See below, al-Bāqillānī, Appendix III. For the distinction between 'traditionist' and 'traditionalist', see Melchert, 'The Adversaries', p. 235, n. 4.
15. Al-Suyūṭī, *Miftāḥ al-janna*, p. 16, para. 7. Some traditionalists identify religion with tradition; according to al-Taymī (*al-Ḥujja*, vol. 1, p. 206), religion means traditions, and in al-Dārimī's view whoever defames traditions defames Islam. *Al-Radd 'alā al-Marīsī*, p. 495.
16. Their attitude towards religion resembles, in some respects, the rationalism of the Enlightenment. See below, p. 41.
17. Cf. Arberry, *Revelation and Reason*, p. 24.
18. Abrahamov, 'Ibn Taymiyya', p. 267. See below, p. 51.
19. Al-Nasafī, *Tabṣirat al-adilla* , vol. 1, p. 453. Cf. Ibn 'Asākir, *Tabyīn*, p. 105f.
20. For al-Ash'arī's proofs of God's existence in his various writings, see D. Gimaret, *La doctrine d'al-Ash'arī*, Paris 1990, pp. 219–34.
21. See below (pp. 36–8), Fakhr al-Din al-Rāzī's proof of prophecy. Abū Ḥanīfa is said to have thought that one can attain the knowledge of God without revelation. Reinhart, *Before Revelation*, p. 11.
22. *Uṣūl*, p. 230, ll. 7–9.
23. The other four are: (1) God's unity (*tawḥīd*); (2) God's justice (*'adl*); (3) the promise (*wa'd*) and the threat (*wa'īd*); (4) the intermediate state of the grave sinner (*manzila bayna al-manzilatayn*). Abrahamov, *al-Qāsim*, pp. 15–55. D. Gimaret, 'Mu'tazila', *EI2*, vol. 7, pp. 783–93. Watt, *The Formative Period*, pp. 228–49.
24. Mānakdīm, *Sharḥ*, pp. 142, 742.

CHAPTER 1: THE FOUNDATIONS OF TRADITIONALISM

1. Al-Lālakā'ī, *Sharḥ uṣūl*, vol. 1, p. 9. Through these sources of knowledge or proofs, man knows what he should know concerning the principles of religion, namely, God's unity, His attributes and the belief in His messengers. The belief in these principles is not characteristic only of

the traditionalists but also of the rationalists. However, the difference lies in the systems used to study them and in their contents. Following the Qur'ān and the Sunna is a theme recorded in many traditions. See, for example, Muḥammad ibn ʿAbdallāh al-Khatīb al-Tabrīzī (fl. the eighth/fourteenth century), *Mishkāt al-Maṣābīḥ*, ed. Muḥammad Nāṣir al-Dīn al-Albānī, Beirut 1961, pp. 51–69. The Qur'ān is sometimes called *sunnat allāh*. Al-Qurṭubī, *al-Bidaʿ*, p. 176.

2. *Al-Ḥujja*, vol. 2, p. 224. In the introduction to his book, al-Taymī points out that his aim in composing this book was to explain the beliefs of the ancient scholars (or the pious Ancestors, *al-salaf*) and the people of the Sunna (*ahl al-sunna*) in order to refute the innovators and to strengthen adherence to the Sunna. Ibid., p. 83f. As a rule, the emphasis is on adherence to the Qur'ān and the Sunna or to the Sunna alone. See, for example, Daiber, 'Ibn Qudāma', p. 109; Ibn Taymiyya, *Naqḍ*, p. 48. It is worth noting that the motive of strengthening the Qur'ān and the Sunna was not always the challenge of reason or other kinds of innovations but also the adherence to jurisprudent literature and as a result neglecting studying the Qur'ān and the Sunna. Al-Baghawī, *Sharḥ al-sunna*, vol. 1, p. 4.
3. Ibn Taymiyya speaks of the divergence of opinions in the rationalist thinkers as a point of weakness in rationalism. Abrahamov, 'Ibn Taymiyya', pp. 259–61. This notion has already been advanced by al-Taymī, who says: 'If you consider the people of the sects and the innovators, you will see that they are scattered and have different views ... You will hardly ever find two of them holding the same view concerning dogma. Some of them accuse others of them of being innovators, moreover they arrive at accusing each other of unbelief; a son accuses his father of being an unbeliever ... You always see them in contest and hatred ...' Al-Taymī, *al-Ḥujja*, vol. 2, p. 225.
4. Al-Lālakā'ī, *Sharḥ uṣūl*, vol. 2, p. 538. The pronoun *mā* here is understood as *mā maṣdariyya* and the verb *ʿamila* as 'he acted'. The pronoun *mā* can be otherwise understood as *ma mawṣūla*, hence the verse would read: 'God has created you and that which you make'. The meaning of the verb *ʿamila* is either 'he acted' or 'he made'. Abrahamov, *al-Qāsim*, p. 46f.
5. Al-Lālakā'ī, ibid., vol. 2, p. 541.
6. Ibid., pp. 580ff.
7. Ibid., pp. 655ff.
8. Al-Barbahārī (a Ḥanbalite scholar d. 329/940), *Sharḥ al-sunna*, p. 24. Abū Yaʿlā, *Ṭabaqāt*, vol. 2, p. 241: 'The Sunna interprets the Qur'ān and serves as its proofs, and there is neither analogy in the Sunna, nor parables apply to it. It is neither perceived by the intellect nor by personal inclinations' (*lā tudraku bi'l-ʿuqūl wa-lā bi'l-ahwā'*).
9. Al-Taymī, *al-Ḥujja*, vol. 1, p. 98f. Al-Lālakā'ī, *Sharḥ uṣūl*, vol. 2, pp. 524–27. Al-Suyūṭī, *Ṣawn*, vol. 1, p. 82f. The verb *tafakkara* means to prove something on the basis of premises. Al-Jurjānī defines *fikr* (literally 'thought') as 'the arrangement of things known in order to obtain the thing unknown' (*tartīb umūr maʿlūma li-tata'addā ilā majhūl*). *Kitāb al-taʿrīfāt*, ed. G. Flügel, Leipzig 1845, p. 176. In *Kitāb al-tafakkur* (*The Book of Reflection*) in *Iḥyā'* (vol. 4, p. 425), al-Ghazālī states: 'Know that the

meaning of discursive knowledge (literally 'reflection' – *tafakkur*) is to bring two pieces of knowledge into the heart in order to derive from both a third piece of knowledge'. Abrahamov, 'Al-Ghazālī's Supreme Way,' p. 161f. See below, p. 9f.

10. Ibn Taymiyya, *Maʿārij al-wuṣūl*, p. 175: 'God's Messenger has explained the whole of religion, its roots and branches, its plain meaning and its hidden one, its knowledge and its practice'. This notion was already introduced in Islamic theology by al-Khaṭṭābī as quoted in al-Suyūṭī's *Ṣawn*, vol. 1, p. 141. The Qur'ānic basis of this notion is *sūra* 5, v. 3: 'Today I have completed your religion for you'. Cf. Al-Rāzī, *Tafsīr*, part XI, p. 139, the fifth issue. This notion is more extreme than the notion expressed by al-Taymī, for al-Taymī allows the use of reason on the condition of its compliance with the Qur'ān and the Sunna.
11. Al-Lālakā'ī, *Sharḥ uṣūl*, vol. 2, pp. 627–33. Abū Yaʿlā, *Ṭabaqāt*, vol. 2, p. 25. See below, p. 10.
12. Abū Yaʿlā, *Ṭabaqāt*, vol. 2, p. 30 (quoting the al-Barbahārī's creed).
13. Al-Dārimī, *al-Radd ʿalā al-jahmiyya*, p. 306. This notion also appears in juristic literature; in his *al-Risāla*, al-Shāfiʿī states that revelation (meaning the Qur'ān and the Sunna; cf. Wansbrough, *Quranic Studies*, p. 174f.) is a necessary, an exclusive and a sufficient source of knowledge. Calder, 'Ikhtilāf and Ijmāʿ', p. 72.
14. The traditionalists believe in the uncreatedness of the Qur'ān, for they regard the Qur'ān as God's speech, which means a divine attribute, and God's attributes are eternal. See below, p. 54. Traditions play an important role in the elevation of the Qur'ān. Rubin, *The Eye of the Beholder*, p. 10. The trustworthiness of the Qur'ān as God's revelation to the Prophet is proved through miracles God did for him, and for later generations it is proved through *khabar mutawātir*.
15. Al-Qāsim ibn Ibrāhīm, *K. al-radd ʿalā al-zindīq al-laʿīn Ibn al-Muqaffaʿ*, in M. Guidi, *La lotta tra l'islam et il manicheismo*, Rome 1927. But while Ibn al-Muqaffaʿ (d. 142/759) was considered as a heretic, like the arch-heretic of the third/ninth century Ibn al-Rāwandī (see below, p. 89), the famous poet Abū al-ʿAlā' al-Maʿarrī (d. 449/1057) remained in the eyes of his Muslim contemporaries a Muslim notwithstanding his criticism of *iʿjāz al-qur'ān* and other principles of religion. He even went so far as to make a clear distinction between religion and intellect. According to him, people are divided into two groups: those who have intellect without religion, and those who have religion without intellect. *Luzūmiyyāt*, Beirut 1983, vol. 2, p. 231. (For al-Maʿarrī, see P. Smoor, *EI2*, vol. 5, pp. 927ff.). It is worth noting that in the writings of the Mutakallimūn, chapters dealing with the proofs of Muḥammad's prophecy and with *iʿjāz al-qur'ān* were mainly directed against other religions. See, for example, al-Bāqillānī, *K. al-tamhīd*, chs 10, 11. For a cautious and delicate estimation of Ibn al-Muqaffaʿ's attitude towards the Qur'ān, see J. van Ess, 'Some Fragments of the *Muʿāraḍat al-qur'ān* Attributed to Ibn al-Muqaffaʿ', *Studia Arabica et Islamica*, Festschrift Iḥsān ʿAbbās, ed. Wadād Al-Qāḍī, Beirut 1981, pp. 151–63.
16. *Sharḥ uṣūl*, vol. 1, p. 83f. Cf. al-Suyūṭī, *Ṣawn*, vol. 1, p. 77: 'We have to learn what has come from God's Messenger, for it has the status of the Qur'ān'. Cf. Goldziher, *Muslim Studies*, vol. 2, ch. 1, p. 31f.

17. *Sharḥ al-sunna*, vol. 1, p. 201f. Cf. al-Ṭabarī, *Tafsīr*, part IV, p. 108. Other verses such as 'Obey God and the Messenger (Qur'ān 3.32, 4.59), in which God represents the Qur'ān and the Messenger the Sunna, and 'Those who denied the Book and that which we have sent with our messengers' (Qur'ān 40.70; 'That which we have sent ...' stands for the Sunna) are cited for the same purpose. It is worth noting that the term *kitāb allāh* (the Book of God) in al-Shāfi'ī's *al-Risāla* refers to all forms of divine revelation. Calder, 'Ikhtilāf and Ijmā'', p. 55.
18. U. Rubin, *The Eye of the Beholder*, p. 6.
19. *Miftāḥ al-janna*, p. 15. In p. 49, al-Suyūṭī clearly rejects the authenticity of this tradition. For a similar tradition, see Chapter 5, p. 44.
20. Ibid., p. 16.
21. Ibid., pp. 17f., 26.
22. Ibid., p. 28: 'I have left among you something that if you adhere to it you will never err, it is God's Book and my (Muḥammad's) Sunna'.
23. Ibid., p. 38.
24. Ibid., p. 105.
25. Ibid., p. 107.
26. Ibid., p. 28. Ibn 'Abd al-Barr, *Jāmi*, vol. 2, p. 1,187. Al-Shāfi'ī states that 'Muḥammad's rulings are God's rulings'. Quoted by Burton (*Introduction*, p. 85) from *K. al-umm*. It is thus no wonder that when one of the four imams of jurisprudence (Abū Ḥanīfa, Mālik, al-Shāfi'ī and Ibn Ḥanbal) expresses a notion which is contradicted by a tradition, he, in Ibn Taymiyya's view, must make excuses for his deviation. These excuses are divided into three kinds: (1) the imam's thought that Muḥammad did not say this tradition; (2) the imam's assumption that the tradition is not relevant to the question discussed; (3) the imam's thought that the judgement of the tradition was cancelled. Ibn Taymiyya, *Raf' al-malām*, p. 18f.
27. Al-Suyūṭī, *Ṣawn*, vol. 1, p. 194f.
28. G. F. Hourani, 'The Basis of Authority of Consensus in Sunnite Islam', in his *Reason and Tradition in Islamic Ethics*, Cambridge 1985, pp. 190–226.
29. Ibid., pp. 197, 200–3. Cf. *Talmud of Jerusalem*, *Pe'ah*, ch. 7, 20c: 'Go out and see what the action of the people is and act likewise'. Tr. Calder, 'Ikhtilāf and Ijmā'', p. 75.
30. Ibid., p. 195.
31. Ibid., pp. 198, 203. In al-Shāfi'ī's view, the common people could not unite on a notion which contradicts the Prophet's statements. Calder, Ibid. This is a slightly different version of the tradition mentioned above.
32. Hourani, ibid., p. 205f. For more verses and traditions in favour of the *ijmā'*, see al-Jaṣṣāṣ, *al-Ijmā'*, pp. 137–51.
33. Al-Jaṣṣāṣ, *al-Ijmā'*, p. 66f. Al-Jaṣṣāṣ brings as an example the proof of the Ḥanafite scholar 'Alā' al-Dīn 'Abd al-'Azīz ibn Aḥmad ibn Muḥammad al-Bukhārī (d. 730/1330). According to him, it is logically proved that the Prophet is the seal of the prophets (*khātam al-anbiyā'*), and that his Law will endure until the Resurrection. Now when there occurred events to which no decisive text of the Qur'ān and the Sunna can apply, the community agreed upon the laws concerning these events.

In such a case, if the community erred and its consensus did not necessitate true knowledge, the succession of the Law in some matters would stop, which means that the Law in its totality is not endurable, which is absurd. Consequently, one should state that *ijmāʿ* is a decisive proof for the endurance of the Law. Al-Jaṣṣāṣ responds to this proof saying that it must be preceded by the premise of the immunity of the community from sin, a premise which is based on the Sunna. Thus this proof is not a rational one. It is worth noting that a rationalist such as ʿAbd al-Jabbār rejects the possibility of demonstrating the authoritativeness of the Consensus through reason. J. Schacht, '*Ijmāʿ*', *EI2*, vol. 3, p. 1023.

34. Hourani, op. cit., p. 194.
35. Ibid., pp. 194, 208.
36. Ibn Ḥazm holds the *Ṣaḥāba*'s *ijmāʿ*. J. Schacht, '*Ijmāʿ*', *EI2*, vol. 3, p. 1023f. Some scholars state that whoever follows the *ijmāʿ* of his contemporary scholars is like whoever follows the *ijmāʿ* of the *Ṣaḥāba* and *Tābiʿūn*. Ibn Taymiyya, *Naqḍ*, p. 146 (quoting Abū al-Ḥasan Muḥammad ibn ʿAbd al-Malik al-Karjī). The first tradition recorded in the Shāfiʿite scholar al-Taymī, in his chapter on the group which escapes perdition (*al-firqa al-nājiya*), points out that this group follows the Prophet and his *Ṣaḥāba*. *Al-Ḥujja*, vol. 2, p. 384.
37. Maṭbaʿat al-Manār, Cairo n.d., vol. 3, pp. 135–42. Cf. ʿAbd al-Raḥmān al-Maḥmūd, *Mawqif Ibn Taymiyya*, vol. 1, pp. 27–31.
38. Al-Lālakāʾī, *Sharḥ uṣūl*, vol. 1, p. 96, n. 1.
39. According to Ibn Taymiyya, *ijmāʿ* is all that which people agree upon, but the *ijmāʿ* which is well established is the *ijmāʿ* of the pious ancestors (*al-salaf al-ṣāliḥ*), for after them there were many divergences and the community was divided. *al-ʿAqīda al-wāsiṭiyya*, p. 26 of the Arabic text. It is evident from the text that Ibn Taymiyya does not reject other kinds of consensus, but thinks that the ancient is the best. Cf. ibid., p. 84, n. 261. Elsewhere (n. 36 above), he compares the consensus of one's contemporary scholars to that of the *Ṣaḥāba*.
40. Ibid., vol. 1, p. 106. A totally different meaning of *jamaʿa* is put forward by al-Lālakāʾī, on the authority of ʿAbd Allāh ibn Masʿūd (d. 32/652). Ibn Masʿūd was asked once what one has to do when one misses the time of prayer, and he answered that one should pray at home. When he was told that in such a case a man misses the public prayer, he said: 'The people (*jumhūr*) of the *jamāʿa* are those who withdraw from the *jamāʿa*. The *jamāʿa* is only what agrees with the obedience to God (*mā wāfaqa ṭāʿat allāh*) even if you are alone.' Al-Lālakāʾī, *Sharḥ uṣūl*, vol. 1, p. 108f. I assume that the linguistic basis of Ibn Masʿūd's statement is the verb *jamaʿa* which means to agree (*jamaʿahu ʿalā kadhā* means 'he agreed with him': *Al-Munjid*, s.v.). However, his interpretation of *jamāʿa* seems to have gained the approval of only the Muʿtazilites. See Chapter 5, p. 48.
41. *Talbīs iblīs*, p. 6f. Cf. Ibn Taymiyya, *Iqtiḍāʾ*, p. 141.
42. *Talbīs iblīs*, ibid.
43. Al-Ājurrī, *al-Sharīʿa*, pp. 3, 7, 54, 67. In a debate between an Ismaʿīlī Dāʿī and a Muʿtazilite, the Muʿtazilite states that the indication of truth is the fact that people do not disagree about it, and anything

which is subject to disagreement is not true. ʿAlī ibn Muḥammad ibn al-Walīd (d. 612/1215), *Dāmigh al-bāṭil wa-ḥatf al-munāḍil*, ed. Muṣṭafā Ghālib, Beirut 1982, vol. II, p. 150.

44. The traditionalists, including Mutakallimūn, such as the Ashʿarites, who adhere to traditional ideas, hold that God's attributes exist in Him as eternal separate spiritual entities, while the Muʿtazilites think that 'God is one' means that no entity exists in His essence and that there is a kind of identity between God and His attributes. Hence, the Muʿtazilites are called by the traditionalists *muʿaṭṭila*, those who cancel God's attributes. For the problem of God's attributes in Islamic theology, see Wolfson, *Kalām*, ch. 2; R. M. Frank, *The Teaching of the Baṣrian School of the Muʿtazila in the Classical Period*, Albany 1978. Here we see an example of the complexity of the problem of rationalism versus traditionalism in Islamic theology. In this subject matter, only the Muʿtazilites remain rationalists in that they conclude their position from rational proofs, whereas other Mutakallimūn, who can be named rationalists in other issues, here adopt the traditionalist stand, that is, their point of departure is traditionalist, and they try to prove it through rational arguments.
45. In the traditionalists' view, the believer's highest reward in the world to come is seeing God. This doctrine is based on Qur'ān verses (e.g. 75.22–3) and on rational arguments (e.g. every existing thing can be seen: since God exists, He can be seen). The opposite view of the rationalists is also based on Qur'ān verses (e.g. 6.103) and on rational arguments (e.g. one can see only corporeal entity; seeing God means that He is a body, for one can see only bodies, and a body is created and the Creator cannot be created). For this issue, see my *Anthropomorphism*, pp. 15–18. Some Mutakallimūn, such as the Ashʿarite Sayf al-Dīn al-Āmidī (631/1233) and al-Ghazālī, accepted the Muʿtazilite view of God's visibility which is understood as one's knowledge of God which exists in one's heart. Ibid., p. 7. Abrahamov, 'Al-Ghazālī Supreme Way', pp. 155–7. In this issue, the main stimulus for the discussion is clearly Qur'ān verses for and against the vision of God.
46. *Shafāʿa* means that Muḥammad, or any other prophet, or an angel or a saint can plead for a sinner so that the latter's punishment will be reduced or cancelled. The Muʿtazilites did not accept this doctrine in this form, claiming that a sinner who does not repent is doomed to eternal punishment in Hell. They held that the *shafāʿa* applies only to those who have already repented. A. J. Wensinck and D. Gimaret, '*Shafāʿa*', *EI2*, vol. 9 , pp. 177–9.
47. Al-Bayhaqī, *Al-Iʿtiqād wa'l-hidāya*, p. 187f. The legitimacy of dissent in juridical matters was established, inter alia, through the famous tradition 'Diversity in my community is a mercy from God'. Goldziher, 'Catholic Tendencies and Particularism in Islam', p. 126f.
48. For the last term, see N. J. Coulson, *A History of Islamic Law*, Edinburgh 1964, index.
49. Ibn ʿAbd al-Barr, *Jāmiʿ*, vol. 2, p. 931f. By *al-dīn* this author means the belief in God, His angels, His books, His messengers and the Resurrection. Cf. Ibn Taymiyya, *Iqtiḍāʾ*, p. 142.
50. Al-Lālakāʾī, *Sharḥ uṣūl*, vol. 1, pp. 173–6. 'What proves that the

traditionists (*ahl al-hadīth*) follow the true way (*'alā al-ḥaqq*) is the fact that if you examine all their works from first to last, their ancient works and modern ones, notwithstanding their different cities and epochs and the distance between their abodes ... you will find them agreeing on the creeds without deviation ... their view is one and their transmission (*naql*) is one. You will not see among them divergency ... If you joined all that which they said and transmitted from their ancestors, you would find it as if it came from one heart ... Is there any clearer proof for the truth than this?' Al-Taymī, *al-Ḥujja*, vol. 2, p. 224f. However, the examination of the creeds which appear in al-Lālakā'ī shows that there are some differences among these creeds and that not all the creeds point out the same theological dogmas. See Appendix I.

51. Dickinson, p. 24f.
52. Al-Lālakā'ī, *Sharḥ uṣūl*, vol. 1, pp. 176–82. For the creed of Abū Zur'a and Abū Ḥātim, see Appendix I.
53. *Ta'wīl*, p. 16. Al-Suyūtī, *Ṣawn*, vol. 1, p. 219.
54. Cf. Dickinson, p. 4.
55. Ibid., p. 6.
56. Ibn Taymiyya, *Naqḍ*, pp. 42–4.
57. Al-Suyūṭī, *Ṣawn*, vol. 1, pp. 69–72.
58. A Companion (*ṣaḥābī*) is whoever associated with the Prophet for a period of a year, or a month, or a day, or an hour, or saw him. The measure of companionship is established in accordance with the duration of association. In any case, the inferior companion is better than one who did not see the Prophet, even if the latter carried out all the good acts. Al-Lālakā'ī, *Sharḥ uṣūl*, vol. 1, p. 160.
59. Ibn Rajab, *Faḍl 'ilm al-salaf*, p. 29f. Ibn Ḥajar al-'Asqalānī, *al-Iṣāba fī tamyīz al-ṣaḥāba*, Beirut n.d. (repr. of Cairo AH 1328), vol. I, pp. 9–12. Cf. Y. Friedmann, 'Finality of Prophethood in Sunni Islam', *Jerusalem Studies in Arabic and Islam* 7 (1986), p. 208f. Muslim scholars have devoted whole chapters to the praises of the Companions (*faḍā'il al-ṣaḥāba*). See, for example, al-Taymī, *al-Ḥujja*, vol. 2, pp. 319–78. Ibn Rajab says quoting al-Awzā'ī (d. 157/774) that knowledge is what the *Ṣaḥāba* have brought, and everything else is not knowledge. *Faḍl 'ilm al-salaf*, p. 33. And Ibn Taymiyya tries to prove logically that the traditionists are the most learned people. In short, this proof runs as follows: Since Muḥammad is the most erudite person, those who know him best, that is, the *Ṣaḥāba* and their followers, must be the most learned people. *Naqḍ*, p. 116f.

According to G. H. A. Juynboll (*Muslim Tradition: Studies in Chronology, Provenance and Authorship of Early Ḥadīth*, Cambridge 1983, pp. 171–6), Ibn Abī Ḥātim al-Rāzī (d. 327/938) was the first scholar who expressed the dogma of the collective reliability of the first generations of Muslims. Cf. Dickinson, p. 118.

A typical statement concerning the attitude towards the *Ṣaḥāba* is the following: 'If you see a man who loves Abū Hurayra, prays to God for him and asks God to have mercy on him, hope for him good and know that he is free from innovations'. Al-Lālakā'ī, *Sharḥ uṣūl*, p. 170. 'The principles of the Sunna in our view (*uṣūl al-sunna 'indana*) are to adhere to the *Ṣaḥāba*' says Ibn Taymiyya (*Naqḍ*, p. 128) quoting Ibn Ḥanbal. The adoration for the traditionists seems to have no limit; sometimes traditions raise the rank of the traditionists above the rank of the angels, the prophets and the martyrs. Al-Suyūṭī, *Ṣawn*, vol. 1, p. 196 (quoting al-Khaṭīb al-Baghdādī's *Sharaf aṣḥāb al-ḥadīth*).

A Mutakallim who repents of his way also serves as a means to praise the traditionists. Al-Walīd al-Karabīsī is said to have bequeathed his sons before his death to follow the traditionists, for truth is with them. Ibid., p. 197.

60. Cf. Makdisi, 'Hanbalite Islam', p. 263.
61. Tr. by W. M. Watt in his *Islamic Creeds: A Selection*, Edinburgh 1994, p. 72. Ibn Ḥanbal stopped relating traditions from the traditionist al-Ḥusayn ibn al-Ḥasan al-Ashqar (d. 208/823–4) when he heard that the latter defamed Abū Bakr and 'Umar. Melchert, 'The Adversaries', p. 237.
62. Al-Lālakā'ī, *Sharḥ uṣūl*, vol. 1, p. 24.
63. Ibid., pp. 23, 25.
64. *Naqḍ*, p. 9. Ibn Taymiyya notes here (p. 16), without proving it, that there is a consensus on praising those who adhere to the teachings of the Sunna.
65. Ibid., pp. 11, 17.
66. I. Goldziher, *Muslim Studies*, vol. 2, pp. 33–7. Al-Qurṭubī, *al-Bida'*, p. 171f. According to Ibn Taymiyya, a notion concerning religion which has no religious proof (meaning Qur'ān, Sunna and Ijmā') is an innovation. *Dar'*, vol. 1, p. 224. Many traditions, such as 'beware of innovations' (*iyyākum wa'l-bida'*) are recorded in the traditionalists' literature. See, for example, al-Qurṭubī, *al-Bida'*, p. 173. Cf. Abū Shāma, *al-Bā'ith*, pp. 24–8. For innovations concerning practices see Abū Shāma, ibid., and Ibn Abī Randaqa, Abū Bakr Muḥammad ibn al-Walīd al-Ṭurṭūshī, *Kitāb al-ḥawādith wa'l-bida'*, ed. Bashīr Muḥammad 'Uyūn, Damascus and Beirut 1991.
67. Al-Suyūṭī, *Ṣawn*, vol. 1, p. 78f.
68. Al-Lālakā'ī, *Sharḥ uṣūl*, vol. 1, pp. 114–50. 'Do not sit with those who adhere to the doctrine of free will (*ahl al-qadar*) and do not dispute with them', ibid., p. 118. 'Do not dispute with the people of controversy' (*aṣḥāb al-khuṣūmāt*), ibid., p. 129. Cf. Ibn al-Jawzī, *Talbīs iblīs*, p. 12f.
69. *al-ma'ṣiya yutābu minhā wa'l-bid'a lā yutābu minhā*. Al-Lālakā'ī, *Sharḥ uṣūl*, p. 132. Al-Qurṭubī, *al-Bida'*, p. 198. 'God does not permit the innovator to repent'. Ibn Baṭṭa, *Sharh*, p. 40 of the Arabic text.
70. 'Beware of whoever sits with an innovator', *Talbīs Iblīs*, p. 14. The formula 'do not sit' (*lā tujālisū*) appears frequently in collections of *ḥadīth*. Wensinck, *Concordance*, vol. 1, p. 358. Al-Qurṭubī, *al-Bida'*, pp. 192ff., 313, n. 2. It is important to note that most of the traditions cited in al-Qurṭubī's chapter 'The prohibition to sit and to associate with the innovators' refers to innovations pertaining to dogma, such as 'do not sit with him, for he is a Mu'tazilite'. Ibid., p. 196.
71. *Talbīs iblīs*, p. 14. Cf. Abū Shāma, *al-Bā'ith*, p. 27.
72. Bishr ibn Ghiyāth (d. 218/833 or 228/842), a Murji'ite theologian known for his dispute with the Mutakallim 'Abd al-'Azīz al-Makkī (d.

240/854) on the nature of the Qur'ān. 'Abd al-'Azīz al-Makkī, *Kitāb al-Ḥayda*, ed. Jamīl Ṣalība, Beirut 1992. *EI2*, vol. 1, p. 1242. For this issue, see below, p. 54.

73. *Talbīs iblīs*, p. 14f. The Ḥadīth literature is replete with notes on the innovations and their degrees in the Muslim sects. See, for example, Abū 'Ubayd al-Qāsim ibn Salām, *K. al-īmān*, ed. Muḥammad Nāṣir al-Dīn al-Albānī, Kuwait 1985, p. 82. The severe attitude towards the innovations is exemplified through traditions which compare the *bid'a* to other calamities. 'It is preferable to me', says the traditionist, 'to see in the mosque fire which I cannot extinguish than to see in it an innovator whom I cannot change.' Al-Qurṭubī, *al-Bida'*, p. 181.
74. See above, p. 2.
75. Al-Lālakā'ī, *Sharḥ uṣūl*, vol. 2, p. 524. Cf. Plato, *Laws*, 821a. See above, p. 2.
76. Ibid., p. 629.
77. Ibid., p. 633. For the term *zandaqa*, see below, pp. 28, 41.
78. Those who affirm man's capability of producing his acts. This term refers mainly to the Mu'tazilites.
79. This can be proven also through the succession of traditions in al-Lālakā'ī, ibid., p. 629f.
80. Ibid., pp. 639–46. For this term, see Chapter 3, n. 65.
81. Ibid., p. 633. I do not know whether this tradition has any historical basis.
82. Ibid., p. 712.
83. Ibid., pp. 730–6.
84. Such as likening God to man (*tashbīh*: ibid., pp. 528–33), not making a decision concerning the question whether the Qur'ān is created or uncreated (Ibid., vol. 1, p. 323), and the belief that the act of reciting the Qur'ān is created. Ibid., p. 349.
85. Al-Suyūṭī, *Miftāḥ al-janna*, p. 127, n. 5.
86. Al-Lālakā'ī, *Sharḥ uṣūl*, vol. 1, p. 123.
87. For this term, see al-Ṭabarī, part I, p. 25f. Wansbrough, *Quranic Studies*, pp. 208–11. A. Rippin, 'Lexicographical Texts and the Qur'ān', in *Approaches to the History of the Interpretation of the Qur'ān*, ed. A. Rippin, Oxford 1988, pp. 167–71.
88. Al-Suyūṭī, *Miftāḥ al-janna*, p. 128.

CHAPTER 2: THE PLACE OF REASON IN TRADITIONALISM

1. On this issue he bases himself on Abū al-Muẓaffar Manṣūr ibn Muḥammad al-Sam'ānī (d. 489/1095), a Ḥanafite then a Shāfi'ite scholar. (On the historical background of his conversion see Madelung, *Religious Trends*, p. 35.) *Al-Ḥujja*, vol. 1, p. 314f. In doing this he was not alone; al-Suyūṭī also quotes the same passage and others from al-Sam'ānī. *Ṣawn*, vol. 1, p. 231. Ibid., p. 234 corresponds to al-Taymī's p. 320.
2. This reminds one of Ibn al-Rāwandī's contention which appears in the disguise of the Barāhima's statement. B. Abrahamov, 'The Barāhima's Enigma, A Search for a New Solution', *Die Welt des Orients* 18 (1987),

pp. 72–91. It seems very probable that al-Taymī had some knowledge of the Barāhima's views as occur in the writings of some theologians, for example al-Bāqillānī, *K. al-tamhīd*, ch. 9. See below. p. 42.

3. Al-Taymī, *al-Ḥujja*, vol. 1, pp. 320–2. Al-Taymī (ibid., quoting one of *ahl al-sunna*) regards the intellect (*'aql*) as divided into three kinds: (1) inborn intellect (*'aql mawlūd maṭbū'*) through which God distinguishes man from animals. God's imposition of precepts on man is turned to this intellect. It has the function of distinction between things (*tamyīz*) and direction of things (*tadbīr*). (The understanding of *'aql* as natural disposition was already advanced by al-Ḥārith al-Muḥāsibī (d. 243/857), who regarded this intellect as a means to know God and what benefits man and what harms him. In his view, knowledge is the outcome of the activity of the intellect. *K. mā'iyat al-'aql*, pp. 201f., 205. Ibn Taymiyya pointed out later that through necessary natural knowledge man knows that God is above and distinct from his creation. This is general knowledge which revelation details and explains. *Naqḍ*, pp. 38f, 52. Even in a traditionalist there is a place for necessary knowledge as proof. Cf. Abrahamov, 'Necessary Knowledge'. Moreover, the notion that one can attain general knowledge through the intellect and that details of this knowledge are supplied by revelation (*al-fiṭra ta'lamu al-amr mujmalan wa'l-sharī'a tufaṣṣiluhu wa-tubayyinuhu*) reminds one of the Mu'tazila's attitude towards moral values. See below, p. 36. Thus Ibn Taymiyya seems to have learned from his bitter adversaries. This shows again that sometimes the boundaries between traditionalists and rationalists cannot be definitely fixed.) (2) Revelational intellect (*'aql al-ta'yīd*) which God gives to the prophets and to pious people. (3) Intellect which is attained through experience and contacts among people. For a distinction between intellect and knowledge, see below, p. 17.
4. Ibid., vol. 2, p. 66.
5. This verse might have served the Ḥanbalite scholar and Ibn Taymiyya's eminent disciple Ibn al-Qayyim al-Jawjiyya (d. 751/1350), who stated that actions are good or evil by virtue of themselves, but reward or punishment are deserved only through God's orders or prohibitions. *Madārij al-Sālikīn*, Beirut 1983, vol. 1, p. 127. Al-Taymī, *al-Ḥujja*, vol. 1, p. 315, n. 2. In expressing such a view, he partly accepts the doctrine of the Mu'tazila concerning the intrinsic value of man's actions. See below, p. 36.

   In the Ash'arite Mutakallim Fakhr al-Dīn al-Rāzī's view, the messenger mentioned in this verse is the intellect through which one affirms the existence of revelation. Had intellect not been sent to man, no prophetic revelation would have existed. *Mafātīḥ al-ghayb*, part XX, p. 172f. Al-Suyūṭī ascribes this notion, as a logical possibility, to all the Mutakallimūn, saying: 'If one said "There is no god but God and my intellect is God's messenger", he would not be considered an unbeliever in the eyes of the Mutakallimun'. *Ṣawn*, vol. 1, p. 232.

   However, we should stress again that all the pure traditionalists share the notion that theological dogmas must be deduced from revelation and not from reason. This is clearly stated by the Mālikite scholar Ibn 'Abd al-Barr (d. 463/1070): 'There is no controversy among the jurisprudents in all the countries and all the people of the Sunna, i.e., the people of jurisprudence and tradition (*ahl al-fiqh wa'l-ḥadīth*) on the denial of analogy (*qiyās*) in the matter of God's unity (*tawḥīd*, which means theological issues; sometimes theology is called 'the knowledge of God's unity' – *'ilm al-tawḥīd*) and on the affirmation of it in the matter of law (*aḥkām*)'. *Jāmi'*, vol. 2, p. 887.

6. Al-Lālakā'ī, *Sharḥ*, vol. 1, pp. 193–203. Cf. al-Taymī, *al-Ḥujja*, vol. 1, p. 314f.
7. In al-Suyūṭī's wording: 'We have given people the intellect only to establish worship and not to perceive Godship (*li-iqāmat al-'ubūdiyya lā li-idrāk al-rubūbiyya*). Whoever uses what he has been given in order to establish worship for the purpose of perceiving Godship, misses worship and does not perceive Godship ... The intellect is a device of distinguishing between good and evil, tradition and innovation, hypocrisy and sincerity. Without the intellect there would not be imposition of precepts (*taklīf*).' *Ṣawn*, vol. 1, p. 233.
8. Cf. H. Lazarus-Yafeh, 'Some Notes on the Term *Taqlīd* in the Writings of al-Ghazzālī', *Israel Oriental Studies* 1 (1971), pp. 249–56. Frank, 'Al-Ghazālī on *Taqlīd*'. For *taqlīd* in Ibn Taymiyya, see Laoust, *Essai*, pp. 226–30.
9. *Al-Ḥujja*, vol. 2, p. 116.
10. Cf. Ibn 'Abd al-Barr (*Jāmi'*, vol. 2, p. 787), who adds to the understanding of this phenomenon saying that sometimes the *muqallid* knows the mistaken view but is afraid to oppose it.
11. Al-Taymī, *al-Ḥujja*, vol. 2, p. 116f. The intellect is a condition of understanding but not its cause, which is God. Al-Suyūṭī, *Ṣawn*, vol. 1, p. 232f.
12. Ibid., p. 117. Cf. Mānakdīm, *Sharḥ*, pp. 39, 69. Al-Lālakā'ī, *Sharḥ uṣūl*, vol. 1, p. 193, n. 1. See Chapter 5.
13. See Chapter 3, n. 23.
14. 'There is no deity but God' (*lā ilāha illā allāhu*) and 'Muḥammad is the Messenger of God' (*wa-muḥammad rasūl allāh*). See D. Gimaret, 'Shahāda', *EI2*, vol. 9, p. 201.
15. A group of theologians whose eponym was Jahm ibn Ṣafwān (d. 128/745). Jahm is said to have denied God's attributes, interpreted anthropomorphic phrases of the Qur'ān figuratively and held strict predestination. Abrahamov, *Anthropomorphism*, pp. 73–5, n. 42.
16. Since if He were in a certain place, for example on the Throne, He would be limited by the Throne and hence be like created beings. Abrahamov, *Anthropomorphism*, p. 9f.
17. *Al-Radd 'alā al-zanādiqa wa'l-jahmiyya*, p. 92f. Cf. al-Dārimī, *al-Radd 'alā al-Marīsī*, p. 453f.
18. For this name see Fakhr al-Dīn al-Rāzī, *Sharḥ asmā' allāh al-ḥusnā*, ed. Ṭaha 'Abd al-Ra'ūf Sa'd, Beirut 1990, pp. 258–60.
19. Al-Ash'arī, *al-Ibāna*, p. 32. Al-Bāqillānī, *K. al-tamhīd*, p. 260.
20. For this argument see J. van Ess, 'The Logical Structure of Islamic Theology', *Logic in Classical Islamic Culture*, ed. G. E. von Grunebaum, Wiesbaden 1970, pp. 40–2.
21. Ibn Ḥanbal, *al-Radd 'alā al-zanādiqa*, p. 95f.
22. Al-Jurjānī, *K. al-ta'rīfāt*, p. 22. The source of this term is Qur'ān 4.83. See al-Rāzī, *Mafātīḥ al-ghayb*, vol. 8, p. 198ff.

23. Al-Lālakā'ī, *Sharḥ*, vol. 1, p. 217f. Cf. al-Taymī, *al-Ḥujja*, vol. 1, p. 227f. 'Abd al-Qādir al-Jilānī (a Ḥanbalite Sufi d. 561/1165), *K. al-ghunya li-ṭālibī ṭarīq al-ḥaqq*, Cairo 1956, p. 60.
24. Al-Lālakā'ī, ibid., p. 218f. *Khalq* is an infinitive (*maṣdar*) of *khalaqa* and as such indicates both the action and the objects of this action. The traditionalists exploit this linguistic phenomenon to support their thesis of the uncreatedness of the Qur'ān.
25. Al-Lālakā'ī, *Sharḥ uṣūl*, vol. 1, p. 221.
26. A *qadarī* is a pejorative name used by the predestinarians against those who believe in free will, for whoever believes in free will ascribes to himself the power to decree (*qadara*) his actions. Al-Ash'arī, *al-Ibāna*, p. 54. Watt, *The Formative Period*, p. 116f. By *ahl al-tawḥīd* the author may mean traditionalists, or traditional Mutakallimūn, for example Ash'arites who oppose the Mu'tazila concerning the issue of God's decree. If the second possibility is right, it is no wonder that a Mutakallim uses reason to refute a Mu'tazilite.
27. Mānakdīm, *Sharḥ*, pp. 323ff.
28. Al-Shirāzī, *K. al-ishāra*, p. 24.
29. Mānakdīm, *Sharḥ*, p. 396.
30. 'The *bi-lā kayfa* Doctrine', p. 371.
31. For an exhaustive discussion of this tradition, see Ibn Taymiyya, *Sharḥ ḥadīth al-nuzūl*, ed. Muḥammad ibn 'Abd al-Raḥmān al-Khamīs, Riyadh 1993.
32. For this term, see al-Jurjānī, *K. al-ta'rīfāt*, p. 245. The argument appears in al-Dārimī, *al-Radd 'alā al-Marīsī*, p. 377f.
33. Al-Dārimī, ibid., p. 380.
34. Abrahamov, 'The *bi-lā kayfa* Doctrine', p. 371.
35. Al-Dārimī, ibid., p. 417.
36. Madelung, *Der Imam*, pp. 112–14. Peters, *God's Created Speech*, p. 248f.
37. Al-Taymī, *al-Ḥujja*, vol. 1, p. 300f.
38. *Al-I'tiqād wa'l-hidāya, p. 52.*
39. *Al-Ḥujja*, vol. 2, p. 502f. For another definition of *'aql*, see above, p. 76, n. 3.
40. Ibid., pp. 504–6.
41. See below, Chapter 3, n. 32.
42. *Ma'ārij al-wuṣūl*, p. 179.
43. Ed. R. J. McCarthy in his *The Theology of al-Ash'arī*, Beirut 1953. Cf. al-Subkī, *Ṭabaqāt*, vol. 3, p. 421: 'One wonders at whoever says that the science of the Kalām does not occur in the Qur'ān'.
44. Ibn al-'Arabī, *Qānūn al-ta'wīl*, pp. 111–14. Ibn al-'Arabī called al-Ghazālī *dānishmand* which means in Persian 'the sage'.
45. Ibid., pp. 176–8.

CHAPTER 3: TRADITIONALISM AGAINST RATIONALISM

1. Qur'ān exegesis naturally contains references to Muslim dogmas, but since this genre as a whole is not dedicated only to theology, I have not included it in this inquiry. Notwithstanding, I have referred from

time to time to Qur'ānic interpretation when it has a direct bearing on a certain issue or a certain thinker.

2. Al-Ṭabarī, *Tafsīr*, part 1, p. 27. Ibn Kathīr, *Tafsīr*, vol. 1, p. 10. I. Goldziher, *Die Richtungen der Islamischen Koranauslegung*, repr. Leiden 1952, 61f., tr. into Arabic by 'Abd al-Ḥalīm al-Najjār, *Madhāhib al-tafsīr al-islāmī*, Cairo 1955, p. 80.
3. I. Goldziher, *The Ẓāhiris*. *Qiyās*, says the Shāfi'ite scholar Abū Ḥāmid Muḥammad al-Maqdisi (d. 888/1483), was first used by the Devil (*iblīs*), who was also the first to create contradiction between the plain meaning of the text (*al-naṣṣ*) and that which is intelligible (*al-ma'qūl*). The Devil refused to obey God's order to bow himself to Adam, arguing that he is better than Adam, for Adam was created of clay, whereas he was created of fire. Qur'ān 17.61, 7.12. The author adds some others logical questions of the Devil. *Al-Risāla fī al-radd 'alā al-rāfiḍa*, ed. 'Abd al-Wahhāb Khalīl al-Raḥmān, Bombay 1983, pp. 124–7. Cf. al-Ṭabarī, *Tafsīr*, part 14, p. 22.
4. See above, p. x.
5. See below, Chapter 6.
6. The main controversy between the two parties concerns the question of belief. Extreme Khārijites claimed that whoever commits a grave sin (*kabīra*) is an unbeliever and doomed to eternal punishment in Hell, which means that one's actions are relevant to one's belief, while extreme Murji'ites claimed that belief is man's knowledge of God, which means that one's actions have no connection to one's belief. Al-Ash'arī, *Maqālāt*, pp. 86, 132.
7. Those who believe in free will as opposed to those who believe in predestination.
8. Those who give precedence to 'Alī as against those who prefer Abū Bakr and 'Umar. *Ta'wīl*, pp. 3–6.
9. See, on him, H. S. Nyberg, *EI2*, vol. 1, pp. 127–9.
10. See, on him, J. van Ess, *EI2*, vol. 7, pp. 1057f. Al-Naẓẓām composed a book on his controversy with Abū al-Hudhayl. Watt, *The Formative Period*, p. 220. One of their controversies revolved round the doctrine of atoms, which Abū al-Hudhayl affirmed while al-Naẓẓām denied. Al-Ash'arī, *Maqālāt*, pp. 314, 318.
11. See, on him, H. S. Nyberg and Khalīl Athāmina, *EI2*, vol. 7, pp. 866–8. Watt, ibid., pp. 199–201. Probably Ibn Qutayba had in mind the theory of *kasb* whose originators were Ḍirār ibn 'Amr (d. 200/815) and al-Ḥusayn ibn Muḥammad al-Najjār (d. 221/836?). This theory opposes the theory of man's choosing his acts adopted by the Mu'tazilites.
12. *Ta'wīl*, pp. 14–16.
13. Ibid., pp. 44–6.
14. *Maqālāt*, p. 5, l. 5.
15. For the refutation of this view, see ibid., p. 46f.
16. *Al-Radd 'alā al-jahmiyya*, p. 308f.
17. J. van Ess, 'Skepticism in Islamic Religious Thought', *Al-Abḥāth* 21 (1968), p. 7.
18. *Naqḍ*, p. 25. The contention that the process of reasoning leads to doubts and hence shakes one's belief in God was already mentioned in al-Māturīdī's *K. al-tawḥīd*. (For al-Māturīdī, see Chapter 5.) He answers

this claim by stating that the intellect's activity is natural and cannot be stopped. Indeed, it is dangerous, but such are man's other activities; one should abstain from its disadvantages and attempt to gain its benefits. Pessagno, 'Intellect', p. 21.

19. *Dar'*, vol. 1, p. 193, quoted in my 'Ibn Taymiyya on the Agreement', p. 259. Cf. *Naqḍ*, pp. 22–44.
20. Abrahamov, ibid., p. 259f.
21. Ibid., p. 260.
22. Ibid. Cf. al-Suyūṭī, *Ṣawn*, vol. 1, p. 220. It is worth noting that one of Ibn ʿAsākir's arguments in his apologia for al-Ashʿarī is the notion that al-Ashʿarī inherited the knowledge of Kalām from his ancestors who are reported to have asked Muḥammad theological questions. *Tabyīn*, p. 105. Thus practising Kalām is justified on account of its having been a tool used by the Prophet himself. Moreover, Ibn ʿAsākir wonders at those who state that *ʿilm al-kalām* does not occur in the Qur'ān. In his view, whoever denies this knowledge is either an ignorant person who inclines to *taqlīd* or a person who adheres to wrong and innovative opinions. Ibid., p. 359. Cf. al-Subkī, *Ṭabaqāt*, vol. 3, p. 421f. Al-Ghazālī denies the possibility that the Prophet has dealt with Kalām proofs, arguing that there is no transmission of such information. *Fayṣal al-tafriqa*, p. 20.
23. See Chapter 6.
24. Abrahamov, 'Ibn Taymiyya on the Agreement', p. 260f.
25. A *ḥadīth mutawātir* is a tradition with many chains of transmitters, all known to be reliable, so that a lie cannot penetrate it. *EI2*, vol. 2, p. 25. Al-Jurjānī, *K. al-taʿrīfāt*, p. 74.
26. Abrahamov, 'Ibn Taymiyya on the Agreement', p. 261. Most of the Muslim theologians consider *khabar mutawātir* as a device which provides necessary and certain knowledge. Abrahamov, 'Necessary Knowledge', p. 22. However, the Ismāʿīlī Dāʿī ʿAlī ibn Muḥammad ibn al-Walīd (d. 612/1215) opposes this view, saying that a great number of people may agree on a lie and their lie will be transmitted afterwards by means of *tawātur*. Furthermore, each Muslim sect bases the trustworthiness of its creeds and arguments on the process of *tawātur*. Now, if *tawātur* causes certain knowledge, whereas the sects have contradictory ideas, one cannot know where the truth exists. Abrahamov, 'An Ismāʿīlī Epistemology: The Case of Al-Dāʿī al-Muṭlaq ʿAlī B. Muḥammad B. al-Walīd', *Journal of Semitic Studies*, 41:2 (1996), pp. 270–2.
27. Al-Suyūṭī, *Ṣawn*, vol. 1, p. 227.
28. Ibn Taymiyya, *Naqḍ*, p. 62.
29. *Dar'*, vol. 1, p. 208f. Quoted in Abrahamov, 'Ibn Taymiyya on the Agreement', p. 261. A similar accusation of mixing truth with error is levelled by Abū Ḥātim al-Rāzī, an Ismāʿīlī Dāʿī, against some of the philosophers whom he called *mutafalsifa* (those who affect to be philosophers). H. Daiber, 'Abū Ḥātim al-Rāzī (10th century AD) on the Unity and Diversity of Religions', *Dialogue and Syncretism, An Interdisciplinary Approach*, ed. J. Gort, H. Vroom, R. Fernhout and A. Wessels, Amsterdam 1989, p. 98. Abrahamov, ibid., p. 262, n. 36.
30. Abrahamov, ibid., p. 262.
31. Abrahamov, ibid., p. 262f. An answer to this contention was already

given by al-Ghazālī (*Iḥyā'*, vol. 1, p. 95f.) and Ibn 'Asākir in his defence of al-Ash'arī. The terms 'atom' (*jawhar*) or 'accident' (*'araḍ*), says Ibn 'Asākir, are not used for the sake of using foreign terms, but rather for the sake of attaining the knowledge of God; the use of them brings people closer to comprehension. There are also other terms which have been used in other fields of Islam, such as 'cause' (*'illa*), 'effect' (*ma'lūl*) and 'analogy' (*qiyās*) in jurisprudence. One cannot say that the use of them by the jurists is an innovation, just as one cannot say that the fact that the ancients have not used them is considered deficiency on the part of them. *Tabyīn*, p. 357f. This argument was later adopted by al-Subkī in his *Ṭabaqāt*, vol. 3, p. 420. A comparison between jurisprudence (*fiqh*) and theology (*kalām*) was made by 'Abd al-Jabbār from another point of view. He says that just as the science of jurisprudence takes general rules which occur in the Qur'ān, elaborates on them and details them, so the science of theology treats general theological ideas in the Qur'ān. *Faḍl al-i'tizāl*, p. 182.

32. Al-Suyūṭī, *Ṣawn*, vol. I, p. 64. Al-Ash'arī's rejoinder to this contention is divided into three parts. First, in a typical Kalām system which turns the adversary's argument against him, he states that 'It is also true that the Prophet never said: "If anyone should inquire into that and discuss it (i.e. the Kalām), regard him as a deviating innovator". So you are constrained to regard yourselves as deviating innovators, since you have discussed something which the Prophet did not discuss ...' (tr. McCarthy in Al-Ash'arī's *al-Luma*, p. 121f.). Secondly, even if the Prophet did not specify certain terms, nevertheless, the Qur'ān mentions them in a general way. For example, the principles of the proof of God's unity from mutual hypothetical prevention (*dalīl al-tamānu*; for this proof see Abrahamov, *Al-Qāsim*, pp. 190–2, n. 89, and below, Chapter 4, n. 28) occur in the Qur'ān. Al-Ash'arī, ibid., p. 89 of the Arabic text. Thirdly, the Prophet did not discuss some theological and juridical issues, because they did not occur in his time, but he did know them. If questions on the doctrine of atoms, for example, had arisen in his time, he would have discussed it in detail. Ibid., p. 94f. of the Arabic text.
33. Abrahamov, 'Ibn Taymiyya on the Agreement', p. 270. Al-Suyūṭī, *Ṣawn*, vol. I, p. 226.
34. Abrahamov, ibid., p. 271.
35. Al-Suyūṭī, *Ṣawn*, vol. I, p. 227.
36. Ibid., p. 230f.
37. Anthropomorphism (*tashbīh*) means likening God to man. Most of the Muslim theologians were not likeners (*mushabbihūn*). Abrahamov, *Anthropomorphism*, introduction.
38. For example, al-Qāsim ibn Ibrāhīm, *Ṣifat al-'arsh wa'l-kursī wa-tafsīruhumā* and a chapter in *Kitāb al-mustarshid*. Ibn Khuzayma, *K. al-tawḥīd*, pp. 101ff. Al-Bayhaqī, *al-I'tiqād*, pp. 89ff.
39. Frank, 'The Neoplatonism', p. 403. In *K. al-majmū*, vol. 1, p. 199, ll. 15–16, 'Abd al-Jabbār states that whatsoever is possible with regard to bodies must be denied of God. Cf. Ibn Ḥazm, *K. al-fiṣal*, vol. 2, p. 122. Abrahamov, *Anthropomorphism*, p. 9, n. 52.
40. Al-Ash'arī, *Maqālāt*, p. 157, ll. 2–4.

41. For further details concerning this verse, see Abrahamov, *Anthropomorphism*, ch. 2. Idem, '*bi-lā Kayfa*', p. 374.
42. Ibn Qudāma, *Taḥrīm al-naẓar*, p. 29. For a survey of Ibn Qudāma's arguments, see J. Pavlin, 'Sunni Kalam and Theological Controversies', *History of Islamic Philosophy*, ed. S. H. Nasr and O. Leaman, London and New York, vol. 1, pp. 113–15.
43. Al-Taymī, *al-Ḥujja*, vol. 2, p. 384.
44. Ibn Qudāma, *Taḥrīm al-naẓar*, p. 30. An opponent would have said that also analogy (*qiyās*) was not ordered by the Prophet, notwithstanding the fact that the jurists employed it. See above, n. 31.
45. *Taḥrīm al-naẓar*, p. 32.
46. *Al-Ḥujja*, vol. 1, pp. 175, 288f. Abrahamov, '*bi-lā Kayfa*', p. 375. For affirmation of the existence of God's attributes, see also Daiber, 'Ibn Qudāma', p. 110.
47. Al-Taymī seems to refer to the method used by some Mutakallimūn who state that just as man knows by virtue of his knowledge so God knows by virtue of His knowledge. Al-Bāqillānī, *al-Tamhīd*, p. 197f.
48. Al-Taymī, *al-Ḥujja*, vol. 1, p. 111.
49. On this method, see above, p. 14. Although the author attacks the Kalām, he, like Ibn Taymiyya, does not refrain from using its methods.
50. Ibn Qudāma, *Taḥrīm al-naẓar*, pp. 30–4, 47.
51. It is also called: *qiyās al-ghā'ib 'alā al-shāhid* (judging what is absent by analogy with what is present). This is a Kalām way of proving God's existence and attributes from His actions observed on earth. *Shāhid* means the present world which is perceived by the senses, whereas *ghā'ib* means the hidden world, namely, things which are not perceived by the senses, mainly God and His attributes. God has created manifest things whose aim is to serve as an indication (*dalīl*) of the hidden ones. One must find the connection (*ta'alluq*) between the manifest and the hidden things, and that is the act of *istidlāl* or *qiyās*. B. Abrahamov, 'Al-Qāsim ibn Ibrāhīm's Argument from Design', *Oriens* 29–30 (1986), p. 279, n. 103.
52. *Taḥrīm al-nazar*, p. 50.
53. He refers here to *asmā' allāh al-ḥusnā* (God's most beautiful names, most of which occur in the Qur'an). There is a controversy among the theologians concerning the origin of God's names. Some of them allow naming God according to rational considerations, whether revelation affirms this or not (al-Bāqillānī's stand), whereas some others (e.g. al-Ghazālī, Fakhr al-Dīn al-Rāzī) state that God's names derive from the Revelation, but His attributes can be learned by means of reason. Fakhr al-Dīn al-Rāzī, *Lawāmi' al-bayyināt*, p. 40. For a list and discussions of these names see al-Ghazālī, *al-Maqṣad al-asnā, sharḥ asmā allāh al-ḥusnā*, ed. Muḥammad Muṣṭafā Abū al-'Alā', Cairo n.d.; Al-Rāzī, ibid.; D. Gimaret, *Les noms divins en islam, exégèse lexicographique et theologique*, Paris 1988.
54. It is to be noted that this argument is a part of the general argument against the use of reason in religious matters, for religion means following what is stated in the Qur'ān, Sunna and the statements of the ancient scholars without comment (*taqlīd*). Cf. al-Barbahārī, *Sharḥ al-sunna*, p. 42, para. 75. In his *Risālat al-istiḥsān* (p. 95, para. 23), al-

Ash'arī rejoins to this argument turning it against the opponent and saying that the Prophet did not state that the Qur'ān was not created, although there are some traditionalists who believe in the uncreatedness of the Qur'ān.

55. Abrahamov, *Al-Qāsim*, p. 36, n. 226. Van Ess, 'The Logical Structure', p. 25f.
56. *Ṣawn*, vol. 1, p. 52.
57. Ibid., pp. 86–124. Mālik, for example, warns the people against innovations whom he identifies with the Kalām. Ibid., p. 96. Abū Ḥanīfa regards the Mutakallimūn's statements as the views of the philosophers. Ibid., p. 99f. (Cf. the statement made by the Christian theologian of the third century, Tertullian: 'Heresies are themselves instigated by philosophy. The same subject matter is discussed over and over again by the heretics and the philosophers ... Unhappy Aristotle! who invented for these men dialectics ...' Tertullian, *On Prescription against Heretics*, ch. 7, quoted by Arberry, *Revelation and Reason*, p. 10.) Similar statements are related on the authority of al-Shāfi'ī (ibid., pp. 103–8) and Ibn Ḥanbal (ibid., p. 108).
58. *Traditionistische Polemik Gegen 'Amr ibn 'Ubaid*, ed. J. van Ess, Beirut 1967.
59. Ibid., p. 12 of the Arabic text. A similar tradition is traced back to al-Shāfi'ī: 'It is better for man to meet God with any sin, except polytheism [*shirk*] than to meet God with something heretical [*shay' min al-hawā*]'. Al-Bayhaqī, *I'tiqād*, p. 193. Cf. al-Baghawī, *Sharḥ al-sunna*, vol. 1, p. 217. Cf. Ibn Abī al-'Izz, *Sharḥ al-'aqīda*, vol. 1, 247. Al-Barbahārī, *Sharḥ al-sunna*, p. 54, para. 116, p. 55, para. 117, p. 60, para. 130.
60. *Akhbār 'Amr ibn 'Ubayd*, p. 13 of the Arabic text.
61. Al-Bukhārī, *Khalq af'āl al-'ibād*, p. 130. Al-Barbahārī, *Sharḥ al-sunna*, p. 49, par. 97. God does not accept the innovator's acts of worship, for example prayer, fast, almsgiving and so on. Al-Qurṭubī, *al-Bida'*, p. 158. This Mālikite scholar also states that whoever turns to an innovator turns to destroy Islam. Ibid., p. 159.
62. Al-Bayhaqī, *I'tiqād*, p. 191.
63. Watt, *The Formative Period*, pp. 116–18.
64. Cf. a tradition traced back to al-Ḥasan al-Baṣrī which reads: 'Do not sit in the company of the people of the sects (*ahl al-ahwā'*), do not dispute with them and do not hear from them'. Ibn 'Abd al-Barr, *Jāmi'*, vol. 2, p. 944.
65. Because they admit two owners of power, God and the Devil or God and man. Al-Ash'arī, *al-Ibāna*, p. 54. However, the Mu'tazilites applied this deprecatory name to the believers in predestination (*al-mujbira*), since they shared with the Zoroastrians the belief in God's decree. Mānakdīm, *Sharḥ*, pp. 773ff. The author of *Sharḥ* brings other reasons to this appellation. Cf. al-Zamakhsharī, *al-Minhāj*, p. 61 of the Arabic text.
66. The Murji'a are the theologians who are mainly associated with the notions of suspension of the grave sinner's judgement and of the definition of belief as knowledge. Watt, *The Formative Period*, pp. 119–48.
67. *K. al-ishāra*, p. 45.
68. See, on him, *EI2*, vol. 3, p. 63.
69. Al-Baghawī, *Sharḥ al-sunna*, vol. 1, p. 227.

70. For the development of this term in Muslim religious literature, see Abrahamov, *al-Qāsim*, p. 180f., n. 1. Ibn Abī al-ʿIzz, *Sharḥ al-ʿaqīda*, vol. 1, p. 17. According to a statement traced back to Mālik ibn Anas and to Abū Yūsuf al-Anṣārī, whoever seeks religion through the Kalām becomes an infidel (*man talaba al-dīn bi'l-kalām tazandaqa*). However, in Ibn ʿAsākir's view, here the term Kalām applies to the Kalām of the innovators (*kalām ahl al-bidaʿ*) and not to the Kalām of the traditionalists (*ahl al-sunna*). This is his response to other statements against the Kalām which are traced back to al-Shāfiʿī. *Tabyīn*, pp. 334–7. The Kalām which agrees with the teachings of Qur'ān and the Sunna and which clarifies the true principles of religion when a controversy takes place is praised by the scholars. Abstaining from dealing with the Kalām methods in the period of the Miḥna is explained by Ibn ʿAsākir through the scholars' unwillingness to be involved in debates in the courts of rulers, which can bring about persecutions. Ibid., pp. 348–51. Alternatively, he says that if one engages only in the Kalām and abandons the learning of the Law and also does not carry out the precepts, one becomes an infidel. *Tabyīn*, p. 334. Al-Suyūṭī, quotes a question, to the contents of which he does not agree, from which one learns the value of the Kalām as a good innovation, for it fights the unbelievers and the heretics, distinguishes between truth and lie, cancels man's doubts and supplies proofs for the trustworthiness of the Prophet and other religious principles. *Ṣawn*, vol. 1, p. 209f. As we have shown (see above, pp. 13ff.), the use of Kalām systems of discussion was not carried out only by professional theologians, but also by scholars from different systems of thought, Shāfiʿites, Mālikites, Ṣūfis. Cf. Frank, *Al-Ghazālī on Taqlīd*, p. 218. However, in many cases, what was learned through the Kalām did not serve as the basis of religious principles, but rather as a corroboration for what was already known through *taqlīd*. ʿAbd al-Jabbār explains that those who name the Kalām an innovation do so out of ignorance; whoever does not know something, hates it. *Faḍl al-iʿtizāl*, p. 184.
71. Ibn Abī al-ʿIzz, *Sharḥ al-ʿaqīda*, vol. 1, pp. 17f., 247. One should note the possibility that both al-Anṣārī's stand and al-Shāfiʿī's are not authentic and may be a projection of the ideas of later generations in order to garner legitimation from the ancients, a phenomenon which is well known in Islamic religious literature. Anyhow, we can say confidently that the tendency to discredit the Kalām is evident in classical Islam at least in later generations. Likewise, al-Shāfiʿī is depicted as favouring *ʿilm al-kalām*. E. Chaumont, 'Al-Shāfiʿī', *EI2*, vol. 9, p. 183.
72. *Sharḥ al-sunna*, vol. 1, p. 228.
73. Among his works there is *Maʿālim al-sunan fī sharḥ kitāb al-sunan li-abī da'ūd*.
74. This is also the view of al-Shāfi'ī. Al-Baghawī, ibid.
75. Al-Baghawī, ibid., p. 229. This stand is contrary to Ibn Taymiyya's statement that *ahl al-sunna* neither declare a Muslim an unbeliever on account of a sin nor prevent people from praying behind him. A Muslim should be a friend of his co-religionist, not an enemy. *Rasā'il wa-fatāwā shaykn al-islām*, ed. Muḥammad Rashīd Riḍā, Cairo 1992 (repr.), vol. 2, part 5, pp. 241–4.

76. Al-Baghawī, *Sharḥ al-sunna*, p. 219.
77. Ibn Abī al-ʿIzz, *Sharḥ al-ʿaqīda*, vol. 1, p. 235.
78. According to al-Suyūṭī, scholars who lived before al-Shāfiʿī and al-Shāfiʿī himself maintained that the cause of innovations was ignorance of the language. As an example, the author brings a discussion on the obligatoriness of punishing the sinner (*wujūb ʿadhāb al-fāsiq*) between the Muʿtazilite ʿAmr ibn ʿUbayd (d. 144/761) and a certain Abū ʿAmr ibn al-ʿAlāʾ. The Muʿtazilites hold that if a man deserves a punishment because of a sin and he does not repent, the punishment will necessarily occur. ʿAmr bases this notion on the verse which seems to show that God does not break his threat, understanding the word *mīʿād* in *inna allāh lā yukhlifu al-mīʿād* ('God will not break his promise', Qur'ān 13.31) as 'threat' and not as 'promise'. ʿAmr was accused of ignorance of the language, and this ignorance was ascribed to his being non-Arab (his father came from Balkh). *Ṣawn*, vol. 1, p. 55f. According to ʿAbd al-Jabbār, scholars must know the language and its grammar in order to understand what God and the Prophet have said. However, knowledge of the language is needed only for the knowledge of the laws (*al-sharāʾiʿ*), for the other three principles of religion, namely, God's unity, His justice and Prophecies, are known through the intellect. *Al-Mukhtaṣar fī uṣūl al-dīn*, in *Rasāʾil al-ʿadl waʾl-tawḥīd*, part 1, p. 199.
79. Al-Taymī, *al-Ḥujja*, vol. 1, pp. 306–10. The eminent Ḥanafite scholar Abū al-ʿAbbās, known as Qāḍī al-ʿAskar, forbids the reading and learning of the Muʿtazilite works, for these cause people to doubt their religion, to weaken their belief and to become innovators. Ibn ʿAsākir, *Tabyīn*, p. 139.
80. Al-Taymī, *al-Ḥujja*, vol. 1, p. 371f. Al-Khaṭṭābī's answer also appears in al-Suyūṭī (*Ṣawn*, vol. 1, pp. 137–47) in a detailed manner.
81. Al-Taymī, ibid., p. 372.
82. Ibid., p. 373.
83. Cf. above, n. 57.
84. Al-Taymī, ibid., p. 374f. This notion was developed later on by Ibn Taymiyya in his *Maʿārij al-wuṣūl* (p. 175). See above, Chapter 1, n. 10. For al-Ghazālī's attitude towards the Kalām, see Frank, *Al-Ghazālī and the Ashʿarite School*, ch. 2.

CHAPTER 4: THE FOUNDATIONS OF RATIONALISM

1. Mānakdīm, *Sharḥ*, p. 39. For the term *naẓar* in the Baṣra school of the Muʿtazila, see Peters, *God's Created Speech*, pp. 15, 57–61.
2. Al-Rāzī, *al-Maḥṣūl*, p. 126f.
3. Peters, ibid., p. 63f. Contrary to this position, the Ashʿarites teach that the obligation of theological inquiry derives from the Revelation. Frank, *al-Ghazālī*, p. 34f. Al-Suyūṭī responds to the rationalist notion expressing the stock argument to the effect that the ancient scholars did not mention the idea that man's first obligation is to speculate on God. It is inconceivable that these scholars should not have known man's first obligation. According to traditions based on *tawātur* (see

above), the Prophet urged the unbelievers to embrace Islam and to say the two testimonies (*shahādatayn*) and not to speculate. Moreover, speculation is not appropriate to most of the people; against one who succeeds in his speculation, there are many who fail and become innovators and unbelievers. *Ṣawn*, vol. 1, pp. 224–6.

4. This is a critical commentary of the Zaydite Mānakdīm (Aḥmad ibn Abī Hāshim al-Ḥusaynī, d. 426/1034) on the commentary (*Sharḥ al-uṣūl al-khamsa*) written by ʿAbd al-Jabbār on his own treatise *Kitāb al-uṣūl al-khamsa*. In some manuscripts, Mānakdīm's commentary is entitled *Taʿlīq sharḥ al-uṣūl al-khamsa*. D. Gimaret, 'Les Uṣūl al-Khamsa du Qāḍī ʿAbd al-Ǧabbār et leurs commentaires', *Annales Islamologiques* 15 (1979), pp. 47–96.
5. Mānakdām, ibid., p. 88f. See Appendix III. According to ʿAbd al-Jabbār, the truth of revelation and also of the Sunna and the *ijmāʿ* should be known through the intellect. Peters, *God's Created Speech*, p. 95. ʿAbd al-Jabbār, *Faḍl al-iʿtizāl*, p. 139. Abd al-Jabbār learns that the obligation to know God can be obtained only through the intellect, because other ways of learning are not sufficient; *taqlīd* does not constitute a way to this knowledge, for both truth and lie can be obtained through it. ʿAbd al-Jabbār, *al-Mukhtaṣar*, p. 199f. Also necessary knowledge (*ʿilm ḍarūri*, in the text *ḍarūra*) and inspiration (*ilhām*) are not useful here, since we know that there are controversies concerning God, His attributes and justice. (Abd al-Jabbār's tacit assumption is that *ilm ḍarūrī* and *ilhām* lead to one truth.) Therefore, what remains is to state that the obligation to know God is obtained only through the intellect. ʿAbd al-Jabbār, *Faḍl al-iʿtizāl*, p. 182f. Cf. al-Zamakhsharī, *al-Minhāj*, p. 66 of the Arabic text. The Ẓāhirite theologian and jurisprudent Ibn Ḥazm also regards reason as prior to revelation in certain issues such as God's existence, unity and eternity. Reason, in his view, helps man to understand the meanings of value terms, but not the full contents of them, and also to know some general facts of human psychology. G. F. Hourani, 'Reason and Revelation in Ibn Ḥazm's Ethical Thought', in his *Reason and Tradition in Islamic Ethics*, Cambridge 1985, pp. 167–89. This resembles the stand adopted by al-Māturīdī (d. 333/944; on him and the theological school named after him, see W. Madelung, 'al-Māturīdī' and 'Māturīdiyya', *EI2*, vol. 7, pp. 846–8), who states that religion is known through intellectual argument (*ḥujja ʿaqliyya*) which shows the trustworthiness of the teacher and proof (*burhān*) of the objective truth (*ḥaqq*) of the contents of religion. Pessagno, 'Intellect', p. 20. Cf. Madelung, 'The Spread of Māturīdism', p. 118, n. 30.
6. For this purpose, the reader may consult H. A. Davidson's thorough and profound work *Proofs for Eternity, Creation and the Existence of God in Medieval Islamic and Jewish Philosophy*, Oxford 1987.
7. Ibid., p. 117. For other theologians who used this proof in its different forms, see ibid., pp. 119–21.
8. Mānakdīm, *Sharḥ*, p. 95. Davidson, *Proofs*, pp. 134–46.
9. Davidson, ibid., pp. 146–53. Abrahamov, *al-Qasim*, p. 2.
10. Davidson, ibid., pp. 174–212. Abrahamov, ibid., p. 3.
11. Davidson, ibid., pp. 213–36. Abrahamov, ibid., pp. 1–13.

12. For example, Al-Bāqillānī, *al-Tamhīd*, pp. 22ff. Al-Juwaynī, *al-Irshād*, pp. 39ff. Al-Baghddī, *Uṣūl*, pp. 33ff.
13. Gimaret, *La doctrine d'al-Ash'arī*, p. 213. Cf. Al-Rāzī, *Muḥaṣṣal*, p. 134.
14. Al-Baghdādī, *Uṣūl*, p. 256f. Al-Nasafī, *Tabṣirat al-adilla*, vol. 2, p. 452. See Appendix II. Reinhart, *Before Revelation*, p. 19. Frank, *Al-Ghazālī and the Ash'arite School*, p. 5f.
15. Mānakdīm, *Sharḥ*, p. 151.
16. Ibid., p. 156.
17. Ibid., p. 161.
18. Al-Bāqillānī, *al-Tamhīd*, p. 197.
19. Quoting Ibn Manda, Abū 'Abdallāh Muḥammad ibn Isḥāq (d. 395/1004), al-Taymī says: 'Traditions concerning God's attributes have been transmitted from the Prophet through *tawātur*. These traditions are compatible with God's Book. Al-Taymī, *al-Ḥujja*, vol. 1, p. 91. 'God has described himself as being hearing and seeing and said: "There is nothing like Him; He is the All-hearing, the All-seeing (Qur'ān 42.11)". He had informed that He hears all the voices from all directions. He has not ceased to hear and see and He will never cease to hear and see.' Ibid., p. 94.
20. Wolfson, *Kalam*, p. 132. Abrahamov, *al-Qāsim*, p. 21.
21. Schmidtke, *al-Ḥillī*, p. 166f.
22. The Qur'ān mentions God's knowledge (*'ilm*, e.g. Qur'ān 4.166, 2.255) and power (*quwwa*, e.g. Qur'ān 51.58, 41.15).
23. Abrahamov, *al-Qāsim*, p. 37, n. 229.
24. Abrahamov, 'A Re-examination', pp. 210–21.
25. *Sharḥ*, vol. 2, pp. 639, 650–2.
26. Ibid., vol. 1, pp. 242–8. According to Ibn Abī al-'Izz, some eminent scholars of the Kalām, such as al-Ghazālī, al-Shahrastānī and al-Juwaynī, have regretted their preoccupation with the Kalām. Ibid., pp. 243–5.
27. Ibid., vol. 1, p. 39f.
28. Abrahamov, *al-Qāsim*, pp. 190–2, n. 89. See above, Chapter 3, n. 32.
29. R. M. Frank, 'Several Fundamental Assumptions of the Baṣra School of the Mu'tazila', *Studia Islamica* 33 (1971), pp. 5–18. Idem, 'Reason and Revealed Law: A Sample of Parallels and Divergences in Kalām and Falsafa', *Recherches d'Islamologie – Recueil d'articles offert à George C. Anawati et Louis Gardet par leurs collègues et amis*, Louvain 1978, pp. 124–9. Idem, *al-Ghazālī and the Ash'arite School*, p. 32. Reinhart, *Before Revelation*, p. 13. G. F. Hourani, 'The Rationalist Ethics of 'Abd al-Jabbār', in his *Reason and Tradition in Islamic Ethics*, pp. 98–108. It is important to note that almost all the eminent Shāfi'itie theologians beginning with two generations after al-Anmātī (d. 288/900) considered the intellect as a source of knowledge. Al-Qaffāl (365/976) seems to have been influenced by the Mu'tazilites in this subject matter. Reinhart, ibid., p. 17ff. One of the exceptions is Abū Sa'īd 'Abd al-Raḥmān al-Naysābūrī (known as al-Mutawallī al-Shāfi'ī, d. 478/1085), who says: 'Only Revelation obliges man, and before Revelation there was no rule'. *Al-Ghunya fī uṣūl al-dīn*, ed. 'Imād al-Dīn Aḥmad Ḥaydar, Beirut 1987, p. 138. Also among the Mutakallimūn of *ahl al-ḥadīth* we find Abū al-'Abbās al-Qalānisī (fl. in the second half of the third/ninth century), who held rational imposition of duties (*taklīf 'aqlī*) and the possibility to know

good and evil by means of reason. D. Gimaret, 'Cet autre théologien Sunnite: Abū L-'Abbās Al-Qalānisī', *Journal Asiatique*, 277:3–4 (1989), p. 257.

30. Schmidtke, *al-Ḥillī*, pp. 99–103. Al-Bāqillānī (*al-Taqrīb wa'l-irshād*, vol. 1, p. 281) proves that reason cannot show ethical values. By reason we may mean either necessary knowledge (*ḍarūrat al-'aql*) or speculation (*naẓar*). The first possibility is absurd, for necessary knowledge implies that all people would agree on a certain point, which is inconceivable. Also, through speculation people come to different conclusions, or deviate from thinking or cannot think. Thus speculation cannot produce common knowledge on ethical values. The question of whether ethical values have intrinsinc properties was already discussed in Plato's *Euthyphro* (5, 7, 11). Reinhart, *Before Revelation*, p. 10.
31. Mānakdīm, *Sharḥ*, p. 83. 'Abd al-Jabbār, *al-Mughnī*, vol. 11, p. 134. This is also the Māturīdian position according to which God does not act purposelessly, but always according to wisdom (*'alā al-ḥikma*). Pessagno, 'Intellect', p. 22.
32. Abrahamov, ''Abd al-Jabbār's Theory', pp. 41–3.
33. Schmidtke, *al-Ḥillī*, pp. 117–21. Idem, *al-Minhāj*, pp. 68–70 of the Arabic text.
34. According to the Mu'tazilites, the *taklīf* is in force only when man understands its purpose. 'Abd al-Jabbār, *al-Majmū'*, I, ed. J. Houben, p. 10f. Cf. D. E. Sklare, 'Yūsuf al-Baṣīr: Theological Aspects of his Halakhic Works', in *The Jews of Medieval Islam: Community, Society and Identity*, ed. Daniel Frank, Leiden 1995, p. 262. It is to be noted that in all these questions I do not intend to enter into the petty details of divergences among the Mu'tazilite scholars, since they do not contribute more relevant information.
35. Schmidtke, *al-Ḥillī*, p. 117.
36. Cf. Schmidtke, ibid, p. 148.
37. Cf. *Rasā'il ikhwān al-ṣafā'*, vol. 4, pp. 276–81. It seems very probable that al-Rāzī was influenced in this premise by the teachings of the *Ikhwān*. The notion that all the existents are divided into grades which are connected to each other also appears in the *Muqaddima* of Ibn Khaldūn (Dār al-Fikr, n.p. n.d.), p. 9 (the beginning of the chapter on prophecy).
38. *Al-nubūwwāt*, pp. 171–6.
39. On account of using rational proofs, the theologians were sometimes compelled to accept philosophical theses. W. Madelung, 'The Late Mu'tazila and Determinism: The Philosophers' Trap', *Yad Nama* in memoria di Alessandro Bausani, Rome 1991, pp. 245–57.
40. *Al-nubūwwāt*, pp. 177–82.
41. Ibid., p. 182.
42. Schmidtke, *al-Ḥillī*, p. 151f. Also al-Rāzī admits that some actions such as the beneficient's are known as good and the maleficient's are known as bad due to the decision of reason without the help of revelation. *Al-maṭālib al-'āliya*, vol. 3, p. 289f.
43. Ibn Sīnā, *K. al-Najāt*, ed. M. Fakhrī, pp. 326ff.
44. See, for example, the creed of Aḥmad ibn Ḥanbal in al-Lālakā'ī, *Sharḥ uṣūl*, vol. 1, p. 158. Cf. al-Baghdādī, *Uṣūl*, pp. 245–6.

45. According to the Shī'ite Muḥammad ibn al-Ḥasan al-Ṭūsī (d. 460/1067), they are so called because they are detested by the tormented person: *al-Iqtiṣād*, p. 221. They are the angels of death. A. J. Wensinck, 'Munkar wa-Nakīr', *EI2*, vol. 7, p. 576f.
46. Al-Ṭūsī notes that one must not take into consideration 'Amr's view, since it came after a consensus on the belief in this dogma had been achieved. Ibid., p. 219. But according to 'Abd al-Jabbār, the denial of *'adhāb al-qabr* was ascribed to the Mu'tazilites because Ḍirār ibn 'Amr was the first to deny this doctrine and he was one of (the Mu'tazilite) Wāṣil ibn 'Aṭā''s followers. *Faḍl al-I'tizāl*, p. 201.
47. Mānakdīm, *Sharḥ*, p. 733.
48. Ibid., p. 730f.
49. Ibid., p. 731, l. 1 to p. 732, l. 1.
50. Ibid., p. 732.
51. Cf. Abrahamov, 'A Re-examination', p. 219.
52. For the description of the Balance, its actions and related topics, see al-Ghazālī, *Iḥyā'*, IV, pp. 520–4. Al-Qurṭubī, *al-Tadhkira fī aḥwāl al-mawtā wa-umūr al-ākhira*, Cairo 1980.
53. Mānakdīm seems to regard light and darkness as bodies and not as accidents.
54. Mānakdīm, *Sharḥ*, p. 735.
55. Al-Ghazālī, *Iḥyā'*, vol. 4, p. 524.
56. Here this term denotes traditionists who accept anthropomorphic traditions as true. Cf. Abrahamov, *al-Qāsim*, p. 188, n. 69.
57. *Sharḥ*, p. 737.

CHAPTER 5: THE RATIONALISTS' CRITICISM OF TRADITIONALISM

1. In Arabic literature, the main representative of the notion that both religion and prophecy are superfluous, because intellect is the sole authority for mankind, is Ibn al-Rāwandī (d. 850 or 900), who used the name of an Indian sect (*al-barāhima*) to disguise his heretical views. Abrahamov, 'The Barāhima's Enigma'. S. Stroumsa, 'The Blinding Emerald: Ibn al-Rāwandī's *Kitāb al-Zumurrud*', *Journal of the American Oriental Society*, 114:2 (1994), pp. 163–85. In the theological Arabic literature from the third/ninth century onwards, this notion appears as the Barāhima's whenever prophecy is dealt with. See, for example, al-Nasafī, *Tabṣirat al-adilla*, vol. 2, p. 444.
2. Al-Bāqillānī, *al-Tamhīd*, pp. 104f. Al-Baghdādī, *Uṣūl*, p. 154f. 'Abd al-Jabbār, *al-Mughnī*, vol. 15.
3. See above, pp. 10, 28. In his interpretation of Qur'ān 3.7 (the fourth issue, *al-mas'ala al-rābi'a*), Fakhr al-Dīn al-Rāzī states that some infidels (*mulḥida*, a term which usually applies to those who reject Islam on philosophical grounds, but also applies to whoever deviates from one of the doctrines of Islam; Abrahamov, *al-Qāsim*, p. 181, n. 2) defame the Qur'ān for containing contradictory verses concerning basic theological issues, such as predestination, man's vision of God, God's place.

4. Ibn Ḥanbal, *al-Radd ʿala al-zanādiqa*, p. 53, n. 1. Cf. S. Stroumsa, 'From Muslim Heresy to Jewish-Muslim Polemics: Ibn al-Rāwandī's Kitāb al-Dāmigh', *JAOS* 107:4 (1987), pp. 767–72.
5. Dickinson, p. 8.
6. *Ta'wīl*, p. 3. For the function of the *ḥadīth* in the controversies among parties in Islam, see I. Goldziher, *Muslim Studies*, vol. 2, ch. 3, pp. 89–125.
7. *Ta'wīl*, pp. 3–8.
8. Examples of such follies are: whoever reads a certain *sūra* or acts in a certain manner will receive in the world to come 70,000 palaces, each with 70,000 rooms, and so on. The raven is a sinner. The lizard was a disobedient Jew. The earth stands on the back of a fish. Ibid., pp. 8–9. On p. 60, Ibn Qutayba says that al-Jāḥiz derided the *ḥadīth* on account of these follies. Ibn Taymiyya shows his integrity when saying that the criticism levelled against the traditionists was sometimes justified, for they based themselves on forged traditions in matters of roots (*uṣūl*) and branches (*furūʿ*) and wrongly interpreted the Qur'ān and the Sunna. *Naqḍ*, p. 22. Notwithstanding, he points out that the traditionists' faults were less harmful than those of the Mutakallimūn. For support, he cites Aḥmad ibn Ḥanbal's dictum: 'A weak tradition is better than a personal opinion of anyone' (*ḍaʿīf al-ḥadīth khayr min ra'y fulān*). Ibid., p. 23.
9. *Ta'wīl*, p. 76.
10. Ibid., pp. 10–12.
11. Ibid, pp. 97–8. Ibn Qutayba brings other examples which the editor includes under the title 'A tradition which is rejected by speculation and speculative argument', *ḥadīth yadfaʿuhu al-naẓar wa-ḥujjat al-naẓar* (instead of *ḥujjat al-ʿaql* [rational argument] in the preceding example). The title is different but the contents are the same. For example, 'The sun and the moon, which will be transformed into bulls, will be thrown into the fire on the Day of Resurrection'. The question is what is their sin? Ibid., p. 101.
12. Ibid., p. 99f.
13. Ibid., p. 154.
14. Ibid., p. 165.
15. Ibid., p. 170.
16. Ibid., p. 187f.
17. Ibid., p. 193. The abrogating verse is Qur'ān 4.4. For the problem of *naskh* [abrogation] concerning the bequest verses, see D. S. Powers, 'On the Abrogation of the Bequest Verses', *Arabica* 29 (1982), pp. 246–95.
18. Ibn Qutayba, *Ta'wīl*, p. 202. For *ajal* in the Muʿtazila, see my 'The Appointed Time of Death (Ağal) according to ʿAbd al-Ğabbār', *Israel Oriental Studies* 13 (1993), pp. 7–38.
19. Ibn Qutayba, ibid., pp. 260, 270.
20. See above, Chapter 1, n. 72.
21. For a discussion of this kind of criticism, see for example *K. al-radd ʿalā al-Marīsī*, pp. 497, 500, 502.
22. Ibid., p. 485.
23. Ibid., p. 492f.
24. Ibid., p. 493.

25. Ibid., p. 508.
26. Ibid., p. 498. Except for the first two words, this is a quotation from Qur'ān 5.91 in which the Devil diverts the people. It is to be noted that what al-Marīsī said may have been ascribed to him wrongly, for the opposition to him probably derived from his being a believer in the creation of the Qur'ān. However, the important point is not whether al-Marīsī expressed such statements or not, but rather the very fact that such arguments against Tradition have existed.
27. For the term *ta'āruf*, see R. M. Frank, *Beings and their Attributes*, Albany 1978, p. 35, n. 36, p. 48, n. 8, p. 81, n. 5.
28. Abd al-Jabbār, *Faḍl al-I'tizāl*, p. 185f.
29. Ibid., pp. 193–5. The same accusations are mentioned in Ibn Taymiyya's *Naqḍ*, p. 22. The traditionalists refer to the Mu'tazilite claims against *khabar al-wāhid* through introducing several arguments. Basing himself on Abū al-Muẓaffar al-Sam'ānī (d. 489/1096), al-Taymī first states that a tradition which was transmitted by trustworthy transmitters and the community accepted it enjoins knowledge in non-practical matters (= theological matters). Notwithstanding the controversies of the different sects in Islam, they all base themselves on this kind of tradition. It is worth noting that 'Abd al-Jabbār uses this argument to deny the authority of the traditions mentioned. Moreover, according to al-Taymī, there is a consensus of the ancients and the moderns on relying on tradition in these issues. If one said that it was forbidden to use these traditions, then all the scholars who used it would be accused of error, which is inconceivable. Also, if one does not accept the statements of the transmitter because he is one, one will not accept the statements of the giver, namely Muḥammad, because he is one. Some examples of the Muslim experience are given to support the author's argumentation. The Prophet has sent single messengers to kings, which proves that knowledge can be obtained through one person. Likewise he has sent spies to many places, for each place one spy, and he has learned from each of them. And a student learns from a teacher. Besides, the traditionists knew their work well; they are the experts in traditions, just as the philologists are the experts in language and the jurisprudents are the experts in jurisprudence. What finally proves the truth of the traditionists' doctrines is the fact that they are homogeneous in contrast to the teachings of the sects. Al-Taymī, *al-Ḥujja*, vol. 2, pp. 214–30. Cf. Al-Suyūṭī, *Ṣawn*, pp. 213–16.
30. *K. al-nakth*, p. 22.
31. Ibid., p. 38.
32. Ibid., p. 86.
33. Ibid., p. 93.
34. Ibid., p. 96. Cf. Ibn Qutayba, *Ta'wīl*, pp. 21, 25.
35. *K. al-nakth*, p. 102.
36. Ibid., p. 108.
37. Abrahamov, *Anthropomorphism*, p. 135, n. 164.
38. See above, p. 5.
39. Ibn Qutayba, *Ta'wīl*, p. 18. According to al-Juwaynī, al-Naẓẓām was the first scholar who rejected the Consensus, then he was followed by

some Rāfiḍite sects. *Al-Burhān fī uṣūl al-fiqh*, vol. 2, p. 675f. Cf. Abū al-Ḥusayn al-Baṣrī, *al-Mu'tamad*, p. 458. Al-Rāzī adds that the Khārijites too denied the authoritativeness of the *ijmā'*. *Al-Maḥsūl*, vol. 2, p. 46. For arguments in favour of and against *ijmā'*, see al-Jaṣṣāṣ, *Ijmā'*.

40. Ibn Qutayba, *Ta'wīl*, p. 18.
41. J. van Ess, 'Abū Esḥāq Naẓẓām', *Encyclopedia Iranica*, 1/1, pp. 275/280. Another question which Muslim scholars raised was the preference of the *Ṣaḥāba*'s consensus to the consensus of other scholars. It is worth noting that Ibn 'Aqīl (d. 513/1119; see, on him, G. Makdisi, *EI2*, vol. 3, p. 699f.), who was influenced during part of his lifetime by Mu'tazilism, expressed the view that there is no reason to prefer the ancient sages to the modern ones. According to him, even Ibn Ḥanbal did not abstain from criticising the *Ṣaḥāba* in matters of law. Ibn 'Aqīl, *K. al-funūn*, ed. G. Makdisi, Beirut 1970, p. XLIX. But as a rule, the Ḥanbalite scholars have preferred the ancient scholars to the modern ones. Laoust, *La Profession*, p. XXIX, n. 62. Abrahamov, 'Ibn Taymiyya on the Agreement', p. 260, n. 29.
42. 'Abd al-Jabbār, *Faḍl al-I'tizāl*, p. 186. For a thorough examination of the Mu'tazila's (mainly 'Abd al-Jabbār's) doctrine of the Consensus, see M. Bernand, 'L'Iğmā' chez 'Abd al-Ğabbār et l'objection d'an-Naẓẓām', *Studia Islamica* 30 (1969), pp. 27–38. Idem, 'Nouvelles remarques sur *l'iğmā'* chez le Qāḍī 'Abd al-Ğabbār', *Arabica* 19 (1972), pp. 78–85. Idem, *L'Accord unanime de la communauté comme fondement des statuts légaux de l'islam d'après Abū al-Ḥusain al-Baṣrī*, Collection Études musulmanes XI, Paris 1970.
43. 'Abd al-Jabbār, *Faḍl al-i'tizāl*, p. 189.
44. Ibid., p. 187f.
45. The custom of running to the mosque is probably based on Qur'ān 62.9: 'O believers, when Proclamation is made for prayer on the Day of Congregation, hasten (or run, *is'aw*) to God's remembrance ...'. However, some interpreters hold that *is'aw* does not mean 'hasten' or 'run' but 'go to'. Burton, *Introduction*, p. 58.
46. Ibn Qutayba, *Ta'wīl*, p. 49.
47. Ibid., p. 60.
48. Ibid. It is not a criticism of the Qur'ān which appears here, but only a kind of interpretation.

CHAPTER 6: COMPROMISE BETWEEN RATIONALISM AND TRADITIONALISM

1. See Appendix III. In Fakhr al-Dīn al-Rāzī's view, the matters of the world to come are divided into two parts: those which are learned through the intellect and those which are learned through Tradition. That the world may be liable to destruction and then to a second creation is a rational issue. Traditional issues in this context are the circumstances of the Resurrection. *Mafātīḥ al-ghayb*, part 1, p. 8.
2. Al-Ghazālī, *Ihyā'*, vol. 1, p. 114.
3. See Chapter 2, p. 18, and my 'Al-Ghazālī's Supreme Way'.
4. H. Lazarus-Yafeh, *Studies in al-Ghazālī*, pp. 382–4.

5. Ibid., p. 385.
6. According to al-Ghazālī, quoting an anonymous Ḥanbalite, even Ibn Ḥanbal used figurative interpretations regarding some anthropomorphic expressions such as 'The Black Stone is God's right hand on the earth'. Ibn Taymiyya, who relates this report, does not trust it. *Sharḥ ḥadīth al-nuzūl*, pp. 203–5. The Māturīdite scholar al-Bazdawī (d. 493/1099) states that Ibn Ḥanbal was a pious man who did not hold anthropomorphism. *Uṣūl al-dīn*, p. 253.
7. *Al-Iqtiṣād fī al-I'tiqād*, ed. I. A. Çubukçu and H. Atay, Ankara 1962, p. 212.
8. Frank, *Al-Ghazālī and the Ash'arite School*, p. 7f.
9. *Al-Qisṭās al-mustaqīm*. See above, p. 18. Cf. Reinhart, *Before Revelation*, p. 158. Peters, *God's Created Speech*, p. 15.
10. 'Imāra, *Rasā'il al-'adl wa'l-tawḥīd*, vol. 2, p. 301f.
11. Al-Zamakhsharī, *al-Kashshāf*, vol. 2, p. 441f.
12. For this term in the Mu'tazilite 'Abd al-Jabbār, see Peters, *God's Created Speech*, pp. 65–8.
13. Ibn Taymiyya, *Rasā'il wa-fatāwā*, vol. 2, part V, p. 45.
14. Ibid., vol. 1, part I, p. 246. Instead of *al-manqūl al-ṣarīḥ*, one should read *al-manqūl al-ṣaḥīḥ*. This notion is stated again and again in his voluminous work *Dar' ta'āruḍ al-'aql wa'l-naql* (The repulsion of the contradiction between reason and tradition) or *Muwāfaqat ṣaḥīḥ al-manqūl li-ṣarīḥ al-ma'qul* (The agreement of the true tradition with clear reason). The term *ṣarīḥ al-'aql* (the plain perception of the intellect) was already used by Fakhr al-Dīn al-Rāzī in his *Ma'ālim uṣūl al-dīn*, ed. Ṭaha 'Abd al-Ra'ūf Sa'd, Cairo n.d., p. 25.
15. Abrahamov, 'Ibn Taymiyya on the Agreement', p. 271f.
16. Ibid., p. 272.
17. See above Chapter 5, p. 35.

CHAPTER 7: SUMMARY

1. For rationalist trends in early Shāfi'ism, see Madelung, *Religious Trends*, p. 28.

APPENDIX I

1. Al-Lālakā'ī, *Sharḥ uṣūl*, vol. 1, pp. 176ff. Blessings of God and the Prophet are omitted. The numbers of sections are mine. For translation of some creeds, see Watt, *Islamic Creeds*.
2. This dogma reflects the opposition to the teaching of the extreme sects of the Murji'a, which state that belief is only saying the *shahāda* and the knowledge of God (Al-Ash'arī, *Maqālāt*, pp. 132ff.), and also to the teaching of Abū Ḥanīfa, who is said to have belonged to the Murji'ites. Wensinck, *The Muslim Creed*, pp. 125, 131ff. Since action is included in belief, belief can increase or decrease.
3. Since the Qur'ān is God's speech and God's speech is one of His attributes, which are not created but eternal, the Qur'ān is not created. The authors seem to mean by 'in all its aspects' the different

expressions of the Qur'ān, that is, whether it is written (in any place), or recited, or learned by heart. Cf. the creed of Ibn Jarīr al-Tabarī, ibid., p. 184. In another version of Abū Ḥātim's creed, quoted by al-Lālakā'ī, it is stated that whoever claims that the Qur'ān is created is an unbeliever (*kāfir*), and also whoever doubts his unbelief is considered an unbeliever. According to Abū Ḥātim, one has to take a stand concerning the Qur'ān; those who do not do so are regarded along with those who say that the recitation of the Qur'ān is created as Jahmites. See below, art. 29. Ibid., p. 181. Abū Thawr Ibrāhīm ibn Khālid al-Kalbī (d. 240/854) points out that it is forbidden to pray behind whoever deems the Qur'ān as created. Ibid., p. 172. This article refutes those who hold that the work of man such as the ink, the paper and the writing are created. *Waṣiyyat Abī Ḥanīfa,* art. 9, Wensinck, *The Muslim Creed,* p. 127. *Al-Rasā'il al-Sab'a,* p. 82f. For discussions of this issue, see W. M. Watt, 'Early Discussions about the Qur'ān', *The Muslim World* 40 (1950), pp. 27–40, 96–105. W. Madelung, 'The Origins of the Controversy concerning the Creation of the Koran', *Orientalia Hispanica* 1 (1974), pp. 504–25.

4. Cf. *Fiqh Akbar,* I, Wensinck, *The Muslim Creed,* p. 103, art. 3. Daiber, *Belief,* pp. 41ff. *Waṣiyyat Abī Ḥanīfa,* Wensinck, *The Muslim Creed,* p. 126, art. 6. *Al-Rasā'il al-Sab'a,* p. 78. The notion that good comes from God whereas evil comes from man and the Devil belongs to the Qadarites. M. Schwarz, 'The Letter of al-Ḥasan al-Baṣrī', *Oriens* 20 (1972), pp. 19–22. J. van Ess, 'Qadariyya', *EI2*, vol. 4, pp. 368–72.

   In all the creeds which I have examined in al-Lālakā'ī's work, the authors do not mention the notion that God *creates* all man's deeds, except in Abī Thawr's (d. 240/854) creed in which the Qadarites are said to have held the view that God does not create man's actions. Ibid., p. 172. In *Waṣiyyat Abī Ḥanīfa* (*The Muslim Creed,* p. 128, art. 11, *Al-Rasā'il al-Sab'a,* p. 84), it is plainly stated, along with the mentioning of God's predetermination, that God creates all man's actions. Probably the traditionalists do not mention God's creation of man's actions, for only whoever refutes the Mutakallimūn knows best that one of the central issues is the creation of man's actions. That the problem of *qadar* was discussed in the third/ninth century from the point of view of creation of man's works is attested in the contemporary theological literature. See, for example, Abrahamov, *Al-Qāsim,* p. 46f.

5. The hierarchy of the first four caliphs is directed against the Shī'ites, who consider 'Alī the best person after Muḥammad. Abū Ja'far al-Ṭūsī, *al-Iqtiṣād,* pp. 316ff. For a similar article, see *Waṣiyyat Abī Ḥanīfa,* Wensinck, *The Muslim Creed,* p. 127, art. 10. *Al-Rasā'il al-sab'a,* p. 84. In *Fiqh Akbar* I (Wensinck, ibid., p. 104, art. 5), the author states: 'We leave the question of 'Uthmān and 'Alī to God who knows the secrets and the hidden things'. Cf. Daiber, *Belief,* p. 50f. *Al-Rasā'il al-sab'a,* p. 5. This is a plain attempt to avoid stating the hierarchy of the first four caliphs.

6. For the attitude towards the *Ṣaḥāba,* see above, pp. 7–9.

7. For the *bi-lā kayfa* doctrine, see my article in *Arabica* 42 (1995), pp. 365–79. This doctrine aims at refuting both the likeners (*mushabbihūn*), those who liken God to the created beings, and the rationalists who interpret

anthropomorphic expressions of the Qur'ān and the Sunna in a figurative way. Cf. *Waṣiyyat Abī Ḥanīfa*, Wensinck, ibid., p. 127, art. 8. *Al-Rasā'il al-sab'a*, p. 81. In *Fiqh Akbar*, art. 9 (Wensinck, ibid., p. 104; cf. Daiber, *Belief*, pp. 112ff; *Al-Rasā'il al-sab'a*, pp. 14ff.), it is stated, very probably against the Mu'tazilites who hold that God is everywhere, that whoever says that he does not know whether God is in Heaven or on the earth is an unbeliever.

8. This creed also appears in the formula of 'meeting God in the world to come' which is based on some Qur'ān verses (e.g. 2.223). *Waṣiyyat Abī Ḥanīfa,* Wensinck, ibid., p. 130, art. 24. *Al-Rasā'il al-sab'a*, p. 97f. Cf. Abrahamov, *Anthropomorphism*, pp. 15–18, 108–45. The rationalists argue that God cannot be seen, for one can see only a body, and since God is not a body He cannot be seen. A slightly different notion, according to which God will speak to the people on the day of Resurrection, appears in al-Lālakā'ī, *Sharḥ uṣūl*, pp. 158 (The creed of Ibn Ḥanbal), 166 (The creed of 'Alī ibn al-Madīni [d. 234/849]). It is based on some Qur'ān verses (e.g. 15.92–3) according to which God will interrogate all the people on the day of Resurrection. Cf. al-Ghazālī, *Iḥyā'*, vol. 4, pp. 517–20 (*ṣifat musā'ala*, The Description of the Interrogation). Al-Ghazālī quotes traditions to the same effect.

9. According to *Waṣiyyat Abī Ḥanīfa* (Wensinck, ibid., p. 129, art. 20; *Al-Rasā'il al-sab'a*, p. 92), both Paradise and Hell exist at present (*wa-humā makhlūkatāni al-āna*). It seems that this is the meaning of the article cited here, for the continuation of the article is identical to the article in the *Waṣiyya*, that is, both of them were created and will never perish. Basing himself on Qur'ān 57.3 ('He is the First and the Last'), Jahm ibn Ṣafwān maintains that God will exist alone as He has been alone before the creation. 'The objects of God's power and knowledge (*maqdūrāt*, *ma'lūmāt*) have an end and also His actions will terminate. Paradise and Hell will perish as well as their people, until God will be the Last, with whom nothing will exist, as He has been the First, with whom nothing has existed.' Al-Ash'arī, *Maqālāt*, p. 164 and also pp. 148–9, 474, 542. Al-Khayyāṭ, *al-Intiṣār*, p. 18. In Fakhr al-Dīn al-Rāzī's *Mafātīḥ al-ghayb* (to Qur'ān 57.3 vol. 29, p. 212), there occur Jahm's speculative arguments one of which places two alternatives; either God knows the movements of the people of Paradise and Hell or He does not know them. If He knows them, He knows their number, and everything which has a fixed number has an end. Hence the movements of the people of Paradise and Hell have an end, and after their termination an eternal non-existence prevails. The possibility of God's being ignorant of their movements is absurd.

10. Contrary to the Mu'tazilite stand that whoever commits a grave sin and does not repent is doomed to eternal punishment in Hell (Abrahamov, *al-Qāsim*, p. 48f., n. 290), the traditionalists make God's mercy a device of changing the sinner's state.

11. After their Judgement, people are led to the Way, which is a bridge above the Hell sharper than a sword and finer than a hair. Whoever was a righteous person in this world will cross the Way and reach Paradise, but whoever was a sinner will stumble and fall into Hell. Al-Ghazālī, *Iḥyā'*, vol. 4, pp. 524–6 (*ṣifat al-ṣirāṭ*, The Description of the Way).

12. Cf. *Waṣiyyat Abī Ḥanīfa,* Wensinck, ibid., p. 130, art. 21. *Al-Rasā'il al-sab'a,* p. 94. Al-Ghazālī, *Iḥyā',* vol. 4, p. 520f. (*ṣifat al-mīzān,* The Description of the Balance).
13. This is the Basin which the Prophet will be given in Paradise. Al-Ājūrī, *al-Sharī'a,* pp. 352–7. Al-Ghazālī, ibid., pp. 528–30. *EI2,* vol. 3, p. 286.
14. Both the traditionalists and the Mu'tazilites believe in the intercession of the Prophet. However, they disagree on the application of it. According to the traditionalists, the Prophet may intercede with God for the sinner who is in Hell, whereas the Mu'tazilites state that he may do so only for the repenter. Mānakdīm, *Sharḥ,* p. 688. In al-Ājūrī's view, the Mu'tazilites hold such a notion, since they rely on the ambiguous verses of the Qur'ān and on their reason instead of relying on traditions. *Al-Sharī'a,* pp. 331–9. Wensinck's statement that the Mu'tazilites rejected all intercession (*The Muslim Creed,* p. 182) is misleading. It is worth noting that not only may Muḥammad intercede with God for the sinner but so too may other prophets, angels, saints, pious scholars, martyrs and any person who has high standing in God's eyes. Al-Ājūrī, ibid., pp. 349–52. Al-Ghazālī, ibid., p. 526.
15. On this dogma, there is general agreement among the Muslims. Ḥusayn Ibn Iskandar al-Ḥanafī, *al-Jawhara al-munīfa fī sharḥ waṣiyyat al-imām al-a'ẓam Abī Ḥanīfa, Al-Rasa'il al-sab'a,* p. 96. Wensinck, *The Muslim Creed,* p. 130.
16. See the following note.
17. Cf. *Fiqh Akbar,* Wensinck, ibid., p. 103, art. 1. Daiber, *Belief,* pp. 33ff. *Waṣiyyat Abī Ḥanīfa,* Wensinck, ibid., p. 125, art. 4. *Al-Rasā'il al-sab'a,* p. 77. Ibn Abī al-'Izz, *Sharḥ,* vol. 2, p. 524. Contrary to the Mu'tazilites, who brand the grave sinner an unbeliever, unless he repents of his sin, and to the Khārijites, who regard the grave sinner as an unbeliever and sometimes even as a pagan, the traditionalists, following the Murji'ites, entrust the judgement of the grave sinner to God and do not exclude him from the Muslim community. Cf. Cook, *Early Muslim Dogma,* chs 5, 7. Watt, *The Formative Period,* p. 126f.
18. This article and the following ones (18–20) deal with the obligation to obey the leaders of the community, be they just or unjust, and to cooperate with them in carrying out precepts for which they are responsible or which are relevant to them, such as the Holy War, the Pilgrimage, giving alms, division of spoils, and the Friday prayer. Al-Lālakā'ī, *Sharḥ,* pp. 160f., 167f., 182f. In the creed of 'Alī ibn al-Madīnī, it is stated that people must have an imam. Ibid., p. 167.
19. Whoever follows the Qur'ān and the Sunna has fixed dogmas which cannot change, therefore one should refrain from dealing with debates and controversies. Cf. ibid., pp. 165, 175.
20. This is again an article aimed against the Khārijites, who excommunicate anyone who commits a grave sin.
21. That is because one cannot know whether his belief is right in the eyes of God. This article is divided into three parts: (1) One should not say that he is a believer, for belief in the present creed is composed of saying and actions, and one cannot be sure that he carries out good deeds. Abū Ḥanīfa's teaching that faith consists only of belief (*taṣdīq*) and knowledge lies in the background of this part. (2) One should say:

'I am a believer, if God wills', for one cannot know what his destiny is. It seems that the first two parts deal with man's status with respect to belief, whereas the third one is a mere declaration; one says that his statement of belief in God is true, that is, one does not refer to his objective status as a believer, but to his subjective estimation. Cf. Al-Rāzī, *Mafātīḥ al-ghayb*, vol. 15, p. 121f. (Qur'ān 8.4). Wensinck, *The Muslim Creed*, pp. 138–40. *Al-Rasā'il al-sab'a*, p. 77.

22. God's foreknowledge impairs man's free will, since if God knows beforehand what one will do, one must act in accordance with God's knowledge, otherwise God has no knowledge of one's acts, which is an absurdity. Most of the Qadarites (we mean by this appellation the groups which were the forerunners of the Mu'tazila) held that God's foreknowledge has the function of remembrance and not of causation. Van Ess, *Anfänge*, p. 116f., pp. 44, 49 of the Arabic text. Cf. Schwarz, 'The Letter', p. 29f.
23. The reason for this appellation is either their holding the view that the Qur'ān is created or generally their cancellation of the attributes. See above, n. 3.
24. This pejorative name is generally applied to them because they rejected the first two caliphs, Abū Bakr and 'Umar. Abrahamov, 'Al-Qāsim ibn Ibrāhīm's Theory of the Imamate', p. 94, n. 70.
25. They are so called probably because they deviate from the teachings of most Muslims concerning the status of the grave sinner, the obligation to rebel against an oppressive leader and so on. Al-Baghdādī, *al-Farq*, p. 45.
26. See n. 3 above.
27. The text here is not in order.
28. Al-Lālakā'ī, *Sharḥ uṣūl*, vol. 1, p. 152 (the creed of Sufyān al-Thawrī [d. 161/778]) and p. 183 (the creed of Sahl al-Tustarī [d. 283/896]). This article appears as follows in *Waṣiyyat Abī Ḥanīfa* (Wensinck, *The Muslim Creed*, p. 129, art. 16. *Al-Rasā'il al-sab'a*, p. 89): 'We confess that the moistening of shoes is obligatory for those who are at home during a day and a night, for travellers during three days and nights. This rule is founded on a tradition. Whosoever should reject it would be in danger of unbelief, this tradition being nearly equivalent to an absolutely reliable report.' The Shī'ites and the Khārijites opposed wiping off the shoes instead of washing the feet as it is ordered in Qur'ān 5.6. Contrary to this practice, the traditionalists introduce pieces of evidence which prove that the Prophet used to wipe off his shoes after the revelation of Qur'ān 5.6. Wensinck, ibid., p. 158. For the development of this article in the schools of law, see ibid., p. 159f.
29. Al-Lālakā'ī, ibid., p. 152 (the creed of Sufyān al-Thawrī). Al-Baghawī, *Sharḥ al-sunna*, vol. 3, p. 54.
30. Al-Lālakā'ī, ibid., p. 154 (the creed of al-Awzā'ī [d. 157/774]), p. 156 (the creed of Aḥmad ibn Ḥanbal [d. 241/855]), p. 180 (the second version of Abū Ḥātim's creed).
31. Ibid., p. 165 (the creed of 'Alī ibn al-Madīnī).
32. Ibid., p. 156 (the creed of Sufyān ibn 'Uyayna [d. 196/811]), p. 158 (the creed of Ibn Ḥanbal), p. 181 (the second version of Abū Ḥātim's creed). Cf. *Fiqh Akbar* I, Wensinck, ibid., p. 104, art. 10. Daiber, *Belief*,

pp. 130ff. *Al-Rasā'il al-sab'a*, p. 16f. *Waṣiyyat Abī Ḥanīfa*, Wensinck, ibid., p. 129, art. 18. *Al-Rasā'il al-sab'a*, p. 91. For the creed itself, see Chapter 4, p. 38.

33. Al-Lālakā'ī, *Sharḥ uṣūl*, p. 158 (the creed of Ibn Ḥanbal).
34. Al-Lālakā'ī, ibid., p. 159 (the creed of Ibn Ḥanbal), p. 166 (the creed of 'Alī ibn al-Madīnī).
35. Al-Lālakā'ī, ibid., p. 159 (the creed of Ibn Ḥanbal), p. 167 (the creed of 'Alī ibn al-Madīnī).
36. Al-Lālakā'ī, ibid., p. 162 (the creed of Ibn Ḥanbal), p. 169 (the creed of 'Alī ibn al-Madīnī). Here, one can fault both Ibn Ḥanbal and 'Alī ibn al-Madīnī for stating definitive criteria concerning God's relationship towards man; they certainly know how God will act in certain circumstances. This resembles the Mu'tazilite view concerning the grave sinner; if he repents, God will forgive him, and if not, God will punish him to eternal sojourn in Hell. In this issue, both the traditionalists and the rationalists know what God will do.
37. Al-Lālakā'ī, ibid., p. 162 (the creed of Ibn Ḥanbal), p. 169 (the creed of 'Alī ibn al-Madīnī). The obligation of stoning the adulterers cancels Qur'ān 24.2, which reads: 'The fornicatress and the fornicator – scourge each one of them a hundred stripes' (tr. Arberry).
38. Al-Lālakā'ī, ibid., p. 163f. (the creed of Ibn Ḥanbal), p. 169f. (the creed of 'Alī ibn al-Madīnī). One of these traditions states that if two Muslims fight against each other both the killer and the killed are doomed to Hell.
39. Al-Lālakā'ī, ibid., p. 165f. 'Alī ibn al-Madīnī connects this statement to the notion that whoever is engaged in disputes and controversies is not reckoned as one of *ahl al-sunna*, even if he is right in his discussion and knows the Sunna.
40. Al-Lālakā'ī, ibid., p. 169 (the creed of 'Alī ibn al-Madīnī), p. 183 (the creed of Sahl al-Tustarī, who says only that one must not defame the Companions).
41. Al-Lālakā'ī, ibid., p. 169 (the creed of 'Alī ibn al-Madīnī).
42. Al-Lālakā'ī, ibid., p. 176 (the creed of al-Bukhārī), p. 183 (the creed of Sahl al-Tustarī). This is an article aimed against civil war (*fitna*).
43. Al-Lālakā'ī, ibid., p. 181 (the second version of Abū Hātim's creed).
44. Al-Lālakā'ī, ibid., p. 185f. (the creed of Ibn Jarīr al-Ṭabarī). For a discussion of the terms 'name', 'object named' and 'the act of naming' (*tasmiya*), see Fakhr al-Dīn al-Rāzī, *Lawāmi' al-bayyināt*, pp. 21–9. According to the Ash'arites, the name is identical to the object named but different from naming. The Mu'tazilites, on the other hand, maintained that the name is not identical to the naming and to the object named. The view that all three terms are different from each other is ascribed to al-Ghazālī and accepted by Fakhr al-Dīn al-Rāzī. Ibid., p. 21. Cf. al-Bāqillānī, *al-Tamhīd*, pp. 227–36. Al-Rāzī proves, for example, that the name is other than the object named through stating that God's names are many, whereas the object named is one. Ibid., p. 22. It seems to me that the author of the creed rejects this kind of discussion because it is a kind of speculative debate which has no practical effect.

APPENDIX II

1. This is a treatise of ʿAbd al-Jabbār (d. between 414–16/1023–5), one of the eminent scholars of the Muʿtazila. See, on him, Peters, *God's Created Speech*, pp. 6–23. In the following, I shall translate some passages from his introduction to the *Mukhtaṣar*. The text was edited by Muḥammad ʿImāra in *Rasāʾil al-ʿadl waʾl-tawḥīd*, Beirut and Cairo 1988, part 1, pp. 197ff.
2. This term can also be rendered as 'theology'.
3. By *tawḥīd*, ʿAbd al-Jabbār means several theological issues: (1) proving the creation of the world; (2) proving the existence of the Creator; (3) explaining the attributes which He deserves; (4) the knowledge of the attributes of the created things which cannot be applied to Him; and (5) proving His unity. Ibid., p. 202.
4. Answering the following question, 'Do you not (meaning the Muʿtazilites) hold five principles in addition to the *tawḥīd* and *ʿadl*, including the promise and the threat (*al-waʿd waʾl-waʿīd*), the intermediate position (*manzila bayna al-manzilatayn*) and the command or the urge to do what is approved and the prohibition against doing what is reprehensible (*al-amr biʾl-maʿrūf waʾl-nahy ʿan al-munkar*)?', ʿAbd al-Jabbār states that these three principles are subsumed under the principle of God's justice (*ʿadl*). Ibid., p. 198.
5. The text has *al-ʿamal biʾl-taqlīd*, which seems to be erroneous.
6. These verses and others of the same contents are also used by philosophers and other thinkers to prove that the Qurʾān urges people to examine existence. See, for example, Ibn Rushd, *Faṣl al-maqāl fīmā bayna al-ḥikma waʾl-sharīʿa min al-ittiṣāl*, ed. Muḥammad ʿImāra, Cairo 1969, p. 22f. Muḥammad ʿAbduh, *al-Aʿmāl al-Kāmila liʾl-imām Muḥammad ʿAbduh*, ed. Muḥammad ʿImāra, Beirut 1972, vol. 3, pp. 278–81.

APPENDIX III

1. These are passages from al-Bāqillānī's *al-Taqrīb waʾl-irshād al-ṣaghīr*, vol. 1, pp. 228ff. Cf. Al-Juwaynī, *al-Burhān*, p. 110, art. 54.
2. The word *aḥkām*, which is usually rendered as 'rules' or 'precepts' must be rendered here as 'principles', for as we shall immediately see, *aḥkām* applies to dogmas and not to religious laws.
3. *aḥdatha* means exactly to bring something into being, and *ḥudūth al-ʿālam* is the fact that the world was brought into being. Very probably, the source of this term stems from verses in the Qurʾān (18.70, 20.113, 21.2, 26.5, 56.1) in which the verb *aḥdatha* occurs with the meaning of 'to bring something new'.
4. Cf. Al-Juwaynī, *al-Irshād*, p. 301.
5. According to al-Bāqillānī, what God orders is good and what He forbids is evil. Thus rational considerations are not involved in evaluating the moral state of man. Cf. Al-Juwaynī, ibid.
6. Cf. Al-Juwaynī, ibid., p. 301, l. 1 to p. 302, ll. 1–4.
7. The following is a translation of a part of this chapter which occurs in the Muʿtazilite Abū al-Husayn al-Baṣrī, *al-Muʿtamad*, vol. 2, p. 886–9.
8. The knowledge that God is one and wise does not serve as a condition

of knowing the soundness of Tradition, for even if there were two wise gods, they would not send a liar as a prophet.

APPENDIX IV

1. This work is ascribed to the Zaydite theologian al-Qāsim ibn Ibrāhīm (d. 246/860). Its authenticity is regarded as suspect by Madelung (*Der Imam*, p. 100). However, for our purpose the question of the genuineness of the treatise is not relevant, because we are concerned only with operation of reason in it. As we shall see, reason occupies the highest place in the description of the roots of law. In the following, some passages of the treatise will be translated. The text appears in ʿImāra's *Rasāʾil al-ʿadl waʾl-tawḥīd*, part 1, pp. 124ff.
2. The author here states that (1) the principle of Consensus occurs in each of these proofs and (2) it derives from each of them.
3. For *tanzīl* as equivalent to *ẓāhir* (plain meaning), see Abrahamov, *Anthropomorphism*, p. 33.
4. For self-evident verses and ambiguous ones, see ibid., pp. 25–9.

ACKNOWLEDGEMENT

I would like to thank Mr David Brauner for correcting my English.

REFERENCES AND ABBREVIATIONS

PRIMARY SOURCES

ʿAbd al-ʿAzīz ibn Yaḥyā al-Kinānī al-Makkī, *Kitāb al-ḥayda*, ed. Jamīl Ṣalība, Beirut 1992. (= ʿAbd al-ʿAzīz al-Makkī, *K. al-ḥayda*)

ʿAbd al-Jabbār ibn Aḥmad al-Asadabādī, *al-Mughnī fī abwāb al-tawḥīd wa'l-ʿadl*, various editors, 16 vols, Cairo 1960–9. (= ʿAbd al-Jabbār, *al-Mughnī*)

– *Kitāb al-majmūʿ fī'l-muḥīt bi'l-taklīf*, ed. J. J. Houben, vol. 1, Beirut 1965. (= ʿAbd al-Jabbār, *K. al-majmūʿ*)

– *Faḍl al-iʿtizāl wa-ṭabaqāt al-muʿtazila*, ed. Fuad Sayyid, Tunis 1986. (= ʿAbd al-Jabbār, *Faḍl al-iʿtizāl*)

– *al-Mukhtaṣar fī uṣūl al-dīn*, in *Rasā'il al-ʿadl wa'l-tawḥīd*, Cairo 1988, part 1, pp. 197–282. (= ʿAbd al-Jabbār, *al-Mukhtaṣar*)

ʿAbd al-Qādir al-Jīlānī, *Kitāb al-ghunya li-ṭālibī ṭarīq al-ḥaqq*, Cairo 1960.

ʿAbduh, Muḥammad, *Al-Aʿmāl al-kāmila li'l-imām Muḥammad ʿAbduh*, ed. Muḥammad ʿImāra, Beirut 1972.

Abū al-ʿAlā' al-Maʿarrī, *Luzūmiyyāt*, Beirut 1983.

Abū al-Ḥusayn al-Baṣrī, Muḥammad ibn ʿAlī, *Kitāb al-muʿtamad fī uṣūl al-fiqh*, ed. Muḥammad Ḥamīdullah, Damascus 1965. (= Abū al-Ḥusayn al-Baṣrī, *al-Muʿtamad*)

Abū al-Ḥusayn Muḥammad ibn Abī Yaʿlā, *Ṭabaqāt al-Ḥanābila*, ed. Muḥammad Ḥāmid al-Fīqī, Cairo 1957. (Abū Yaʿlā, *Ṭabaqāt*)

Abū al-Layth, Naṣr ibn Muḥammad al-Samarqandī, *Sharḥ al-fiqh al-absaṭ li-Abī Ḥanīfa*, ed. and commentary H. Daiber, *The Islamic Concept of Belief in the 4th/10th Century: Abū l-Laith as-Samarqandī's Commentary on Abū Ḥanīfa (died 150/767) al-Fiqh al-Absaṭ*, Tokyo 1995. (= Daiber, *Belief*)

Abū Shāma, ʿAbd al-Raḥmān ibn Ismāʿīl, *al-Bāʿith ʿalā inkār al-bidaʿ wa'l-ḥawādith*, ed. ʿĀdil ʿAbd al-Munʿim Abū al-ʿAbbās, Cairo 1988. (= Abū Shāma, *al-Bāʿith*)

Abū Ṭālib al-Makkī, Muḥammad ibn ʿAlī ibn ʿAṭiyya, *Qūt al-qulūb fī muʿāmalat al-maḥbūb wa-waṣf ṭarīq al-murīd ilā maqām al-tawḥīd*, Cairo 1961. (= Abū Ṭālib al-Makkī, *Qūt al-qulūb*)

Abū ʿUbayd al-Qāsim ibn Salām, *Kitāb al-īmān*, ed. Muḥammad Nāṣir al-Dīn al-Albānī, Kuwait 1985.

Al-Ājurrī, Abū Bakr Muḥammad ibn al-Ḥusayn, *al-Sharīʿa*, ed. Muḥammad Ḥāmid al-Fiqī, Beirut 1983. (= al-Ājurrī, *al-Sharīʿa*)

ʿAlī ibn Muḥammad ibn al-Walīd, *Dāmigh al-bāṭil wa-ḥatf al-munāḍil*, ed. Muṣṭafā Ghālib, Beirut 1982.

'Aqā'id al-salaf, ed. 'Alī Sāmī al-Nashshār and 'Ammār al-Ṭālibī, Alexandria 1971.

Al-Ash'arī, Abū al-Ḥasan 'Alī ibn Ismā'īl, *al-Ibāna 'an uṣūl al-diyāna*, Idārat al-Ṭibā'a al-Munīriyya, Cairo n.d. (= al-Ash'arī, *al-Ibāna*)

– *Kitāb al-luma' fī'l-radd 'alā ahl al-zaygh wa'l-bida'*, ed. and tr. R. J. McCarthy, *The Theology of al-Ash'arī*, Beirut 1953. (= al-Ash'arī, *al-Luma'*)

– *Risālat istiḥsān al-khawḍ fī 'ilm al-kalām*, ed. and tr. R. J. McCarthy, *The Theology of al-Ash'arī*. (= al-Ash'arī, *Risālat istiḥsān*)

Al-Baghawī, Abū Muḥammad al-Ḥusayn ibn Mas'ūd al-Farrā', *Sharḥ al-sunna*, ed. Shu'ayb al-Arnā'ūṭ and Muḥammad Zuhayr al-Shawīsh, Beirut 1983. (= al-Baghawī, *Sharḥ al-sunna*)

Al-Baghdādī, Abū Manṣūr 'Abd al-Qāhir ibn Ṭāhir, *Uṣūl al-dīn*, Istanbul 1928. (= al-Baghdādī, *Uṣūl*)

Al-Bāqillānī, Abū Bakr Muḥammad ibn al-Ṭayyib, *Kitāb al-tamhīd*, ed. R. J. McCarthy, Beirut 1957. (= al-Bāqillānī, *al-Tamhīd*)

– *al-Taqrīb wa'l-irshād al-saghīr*, ed. 'Abd al-Ḥamīd ibn 'Alī, al-Qasīm 1993. (= al-Bāqillānī, *al-Taqrīb*)

Al-Barbahārī, Abū Muḥammad al-Ḥasan ibn 'Alī, *Kitāb sharḥ al-sunna*, ed. Muḥammad ibn Sa'īd al-Qaḥṭānī, Makka AH 1414 [AD 1993]. (= Al-Barbahārī, *Sharḥ al-sunna*)

Al-Bayhaqī, Abū Bakr Aḥmad ibn al-Ḥusayn, *al-I'tiqād wa'l-hidāya ilā sabīl al-rashād 'alā madhhab al-salaf wa-aṣḥāb al-ḥadīth*, ed. Al-Sayyid al-Jumaylī, Cairo 1988. (= al-Bayhaqī, *al-I'tiqād*)

Al-Bazdawī, Abū al-Yusr Muḥammad ibn Muḥammad, *Kitāb uṣūl al-dīn*, ed. H. P. Linss, Cairo 1963. (= al-Bazdawī, *Uṣūl al-dīn*)

Al-Bukhārī Muḥammad ibn Ismā'īl, *Khalq af'āl al-'ibād*, in *'Aqā'id al-salaf*, Alexandria 1971.

Al-Dāraquṭnī, 'Alī ibn 'Umar, *Akhbār 'Amr ibn Ubayd*, ed., tr. and commentary J. van Ess (*Traditionistische Polemik gegen 'Amr B. Ubaid*), Beirut 1967.

Al-Dārimī, 'Uthmān ibn Sa'īd, *al-Radd 'alā al-jahmiyya*, in *'Aqā'id al-salaf*, Alexandria 1971. (= al-Dārimī, *al-Radd 'ala al-jahmiyya*)

– *al-Radd 'alā al-Marīsī al-'anīd*, in *'Aqā'id al-salaf*, Alexandria 1971. (= al-Dārimī, *al-Radd 'alā al-Marīsī*)

Al-Fārābī on the Perfect State: Abū Naṣr al-Fārābī's Mabādi' Ārā' Ahl al-Madīna al-Fāḍila, ed., tr. and commentary R. Walzer, Oxford 1985.

Al-Ghazālī, Abū Ḥāmid Muḥammad ibn Muḥammad, *Fayṣal al-tafriqa bayna al-islām wa'l-zandaqa*, ed. Muḥammad Badr al-Dīn al-Na'sānī, Cairo 1907. (= al-Ghazālī, *Fayṣal al-tafriqa*)

– *Iḥyā' 'ulūm al-dīn*, Cairo (Al-Maktaba al-Tijāriyya al-Kubrā) n.d. (= al-Ghazālī, *Iḥyā*)

– *al-Maqṣad al-asnā, Sharḥ asmā' allāh al-ḥusnā*, ed. Muḥammad Muṣṭafā Abū al-'Alā', Cairo n.d.

– *Tahāfut al-falāsifa*, tr. S. van den Bergh (*The Incoherence of the Philosophers*), London 1954.

– *al-Iqtiṣād fī'l-i'tiqād*, Cairo (Maktabat al-Ḥusayn al-Tijāriyya) n.d. (= al-Ghazālī, *al-Iqtiṣād*) ed. I. A. Çubukçu and H. Atay, Ankara 1962.

Ibn 'Abd al-Barr, Abū 'Umar Yūsuf, *Jāmi' bayān al-'ilm wa-faḍlihi*, ed. Abū al-Ashbāl al-Zuhayrī, Riyadh 1994. (= Ibn 'Abd al-Barr, *Jāmi'*)

Ibn Abī al-'Izz, 'Alī ibn 'Alī, *Sharḥ al-'aqīda al-taḥāwiyya*, ed. 'Abdallāh ibn 'Abd al-Muḥsin al-Turkī and Shu'ayb al-Arna'ūṭ, Beirut 1991. (= Ibn Abī

al-'Izz, *Sharḥ al-'aqīda*)
Ibn Abī Randaqa, Abū Bakr Muḥammad ibn al-Walīd al-Ṭurṭūshī, *Kitāb al-ḥawādith wa'l-bida'*, ed. Bashīr Muḥammad 'Uyūn, Damascus and Beirut 1991.
Ibn 'Aqīl, *K. al-funūn*, ed. G. Makdisi, Beirut 1970.
Ibn al-'Arabī, Abū Bakr Muḥammad ibn 'Abdallāh, *Qānūn al-ta'wīl*, ed. Muḥammad al-Slimānī, Beirut 1990. (= Ibn al-'Arabī, *Qānūn al-ta'wīl*)
Ibn 'Asākir, Abū al-Qāsim 'Alī ibn al-Ḥasan, *Tabyīn kadhib al-muftarī fīmā nusiba ilā al-imām Abī al-Ḥasan al-Ash'arī*, Beirut 1984. (= Ibn 'Asākir, *Tabyīn*)
Ibn Baṭṭa al-'Ukbarī, Abū 'Abdallāh 'Ubayd 'Allāh ibn Muḥammad, *Kitāb al-sharḥ wa'l-ibāna 'alā uṣūl al-sunna wa'l-diyāna*, ed., tr. and commentary H. Laoust, *La Profession de foi d'Ibn Baṭṭa*, Damascus 1958. (= Ibn Baṭṭa, *Sharḥ*)
Ibn Ḥajar al-'Askalānī, Abū al-Faḍl Aḥmad ibn 'Alī, *al-Iṣāba fī tamyīz al-ṣaḥāba*, Beirut n.d. (repr. of Cairo AH 1328 [AD 1910]).
Ibn Ḥanbal, Aḥmad ibn Muḥammad, *al-Radd 'alā al-zanādiqa wa'l-jahmiyya*, in *'Aqā'id al-salaf*, Alexandria 1971. (= Ibn Ḥanbal, *al-Radd 'ala al-zanādiqa*)
Ibn Ḥazm, Abū Muḥammad 'Alī ibn Aḥmad, *Kitāb al-fiṣal fī al-milal wa'l-ahwā' wa'l-niḥal*, Cairo AH 1321 [AD 1903]. (= Ibn Ḥazm, *K. al-fiṣal*)
Ibn al-Jawzī, Abū al-Faraj 'Abd al-Raḥmān, *Talbīs Iblīs*, Cairo AH 1368 [AD 1948]. (= Ibn al-Jawzī, *Talbīs Iblīs*)
Ibn Kathīr, Abū al-Fidā' Ismā'īl, *Tafsīr al-qur'ān al-'aẓīm*, Beirut 1970. (= Ibn Kathīr, *Tafsīr*)
Ibn Khaldūn, 'Abd al-Raḥmān ibn Muḥammad, *Muqaddima*, Dār al-Fikr, n.p. n.d.
Ibn Khuzayma, Muḥammad ibn Isḥāq, *Kitāb al-tawḥīd wa-ithbāt ṣifāt al-rabb*, ed. Muḥammad Khalīl Harās, Beirut and Cairo 1988.
Ibn al-Qayyim al-Jawziyya, Ibrāhīm ibn Muḥammad, *Madārij al-sālikīn*, Beirut 1983.
Ibn Qudāma al-Maqdisī, 'Abdallāh ibn Aḥmad, *Taḥrīm al-naẓar fī kutub ahl al-kalām*, ed. G. Makdisi, London 1962. (= Ibn Qudāma, *Taḥrīm al-naẓar*)
Ibn Qutayba, Abū Muḥammad 'Abdallāh ibn Muslim, *Ta'wīl mukhtalif al-ḥadīth*, ed. Muḥammad Zuhrī al-Najjār, Cairo 1966. (= Ibn Qutayba, *Ta'wīl*)
Ibn Rajab, 'Abd al-Raḥmān ibn Aḥmad, *Bayān faḍl 'ilm al-salaf 'alā 'ilm al-khalaf*, ed. Muḥammad ibn Naṣīr al-'Ajamī, Kuwait n.d. (= Ibn Rajab, *Faḍl ilm al-salaf*)
Ibn Rushd, Muḥammad ibn Aḥmad, *Tahāfut al-tahāfut*, tr. S. van den Bergh, *The Incoherence of the Philosophers*, London 1954.
– *Faṣl al-maqāl wa-taqrīr mā bayna al-sharī'a wa'l-ḥikma min al-ittiṣāl*, ed. G. F. Hourani, Leiden 1959; ed. Muḥammad 'Imāra, Cairo 1969.
Ibn Sīnā, Abū 'Alī al-Ḥusayn, *Kitāb al-najāt*, ed. Majid Fakhri, Beirut 1985.
Ibn Taymiyya, Abū al-'Abbās Aḥmad, *Kitāb bughyat al-murtād fī'l-radd 'alā al-mutafalsifa wa'l-qarāmiṭa wa'l-bāṭiniyya*, Cairo AH 1329 [AD 1911].
– *Kitāb al-radd 'ala al-manṭiqiyyīn*, ed. Sulaymān al-Nadawī, Bombay 1949.
– *Naqd al-Manṭiq*, ed. Muḥammad Ḥāmid al-Fiqī, Cairo 1951. (= Ibn Taymiyya, *Naqd*)

– *Ma'ārij al-wuṣūl ilā al-ma'rifa anna uṣūl al-dīn wa-furū'ahā qad bayyanahā al-rasūl*, in *Majmū'at al-Rasā'il al-kubrā*, Cairo n.d.
– *Iqtiḍā' al-ṣirāṭ al-mustaqīm mukhālafat aṣḥāb al-jaḥīm*, ed. 'Iṣām al-Dīn al-Sababāṭī, Cairo AH 1412 [AD 1991]. (= Ibn Taymiyya, *Iqtiḍā*) [annotated tr. by M. Muḥammad Umar, *Ibn Taymiyya's Struggle Against Popular Religion*, Paris 1976.]
– *Dar' ta'āruḍ al-'aql wa'l-naql*, ed. Muḥammad Rashād Sālim, Riyadh 1979 (10 vols) (= Ibn Taymiyya, *Dar'*)
– *al-'Aqīda al-wāsiṭiyya*, ed., tr. and commentary H. Laoust, *La Profession de foi d'Ibn Taymiyya*, Paris 1986.
– *Raf' al-malām 'an al-a'imma al-a'lām*, ed. Abū Muṣ'ab Muḥammad Sa'īd al-Badrī, Cairo and Beirut 1991. (= Ibn Taymiyya, *Raf' al-malām*)
– *Rasā'il wa-fatāwā shaykh al-islām*, ed. Muhammad Rashīd Riḍā, Cairo 1992 (repr.).
– *Sharḥ ḥadīth al-nuzūl*, ed. Muḥammad Ibn 'Abd al-Raḥmān al-Khamīs, Riyadh 1993.
Al-Jaṣṣāṣ, Abū Bakr Aḥmad ibn 'Alī, *al-Ijmā'*, ed. Zuhayr Shafīq Kabbī, Beirut 1993. (= al-Jaṣṣāṣ, *al-Ijmā'*)
Al-Jurjānī, 'Alī Ibn Muḥammad, *Kitāb al-ta'rīfāt*, Beirut 1978 (repr. of G. Flügel's Leipzig 1847 edn). (= al-Jurjānī, *K. al-ta'rīfāt*)
Al-Juwaynī, Abū al-Ma'ālī 'Abd al-Mālik ibn 'Abdallāh Imām al-Ḥaramayn, *al-Irshād ilā qawāṭi' al-adilla fī uṣūl al-i'tiqād*, ed. As'ad Tamīm, Beirut 1985. (= al-Juwaynī, *al-Irshād*)
– *al-Burhān fī uṣūl al-fiqh*, ed. 'Abd al-'Aẓīm Muḥammad al-Dīb, al-Manṣūra 1992. (= al-Juwaynī, *al-Burhān*)
Al-Khayyāṭ, Abū al-Ḥusayn 'Abd al-Raḥīm ibn Muḥammad, *Kitāb al-intiṣār wa'l-radd 'alā Ibn al-Rāwandī al-Mulḥid*, ed. H. S. Nyberg, Cairo 1925, with A. A. Nader's tr. into French, Beirut 1957. (= al-Khayyāṭ, *al-Intiṣār*)
Al-Lālakā'ī, Abū al-Qāsim Hibat Allāh ibn al-Ḥasan, *Sharḥ uṣūl i'tiqād ahl al-sunna wa'l-jamā'a min al-kitāb wa'l-sunna wa-ijmā' al-saḥāba wa'l-tābi'īn min ba'dihim*, ed. Aḥmad Sa'd Ḥamdān, Makka AH 1402 [AD 1981]. (= al-Lālakā'ī, *Sharḥ uṣūl*)
Mānakdīm Aḥmad ibn al-Ḥusayn, *Sharḥ al-uṣūl al-khamsa*, ed. 'Abd al-Karīm 'Uthmān (as a work of 'Abd al-Jabbār), Cairo 1965. ('Abd al-Jabbār, *Sharḥ*)
Al-Maqdisī, Abū Ḥāmid Muḥammad (d. 888/1483), *Risāla fī'l-radd 'alā al-rāfiḍa*, ed. 'Abd al-Wahhāb Khalīl al-Raḥmān, Bombay 1983.
Al-Māturīdī, Abū Manṣūr Muḥammad ibn Muḥammad, *Kitāb al-tawḥīd*, ed. Fathallah Kholeif, Beirut 1970. (= al-Māturīdī, *K. al-tawḥīd*)
Al-Muḥāsibī, Abū 'Abd Allāh al-Ḥārith ibn Asad, *Kitāb mā'iyat al-'aql wa-ma'nāhu wa-ikhtilāf al-nās fīhi*, in *al-'Aql wa-fahm al-qur'ān*, ed. Ḥusayn al-Quwwatilī, Beirut 1982. (= al-Muḥāsibī, *K. mā'iyat al-'aql*)
Al-Munjid fī al-lugha wa'l-a'lām, Beirut 1973. (= *al-Munjid*)
al-Nasafī, Abū al-Mu'īn Maymūn ibn Muḥammad, *Tabṣirat al-adilla fī uṣūl al-dīn*, ed. C. Salamé, Damascus 1990.
Al-Naysābūrī, Abū Sa'īd 'Abd al-Raḥmān, *al-Ghunya fī uṣūl al-dīn*, ed. 'Imād al-Dīn Aḥmad Ḥaydar, Beirut 1987.
Al-Naẓẓām, Ibrāhīm ibn Sayyār, *Kitāb al-nakth*, in J. van Ess, *Das Kitāb an-Nakth des Naẓẓām und seine Rezeption im Kitāb al-Futyā des Ǧāḥiẓ*, Göttingen 1972. (= al-Naẓẓām, *K. al-nakth*)

Al-Qāsim ibn Ibrāhīm, *Kitāb al-radd ālā al-zindīq al-la'īn Ibn al-Muqaffa'*, in M. Guidi, *La lotta tra l'islam et il manicheismo*, Rome 1927. (= al-Qāsim, *al-Radd 'alā al-zindīq*)

– *Ṣifat al-'arsh wa'l-kursī wa-tafsīruhumā*, MS Berlin, fos 94b–100b, ed. in B. Abrahamov, *The Theological Epistles of al-Qāsim ibn Ibrāhīm*, unpublished Ph.D. thesis (in Hebrew), Tel Aviv University 1981, vol. 2, pp. 240–86. (= al-Qāsim, *Ṣifat al-'arsh*)

– *Kitāb al-radd 'alā al-mulḥid*, MS Berlin, fos 58b–63b, ed. Muḥammad Yaḥya 'Azzān, Ṣan'ā' 1992. (= al-Qāsim, *al-Radd 'alā al-mulḥid*)

Al-Qinnawjī, Muḥammad Ṣiddīq Ḥasan Khān, *Qatf al-thamar fī bayān 'aqīdat ahl al-athar*, ed. 'Āṣim 'Abdallāh al-Qaryūtī, Beirut 1984.

Al-Qurṭubī, Abū 'Abdallāh Muḥammad ibn Aḥmad, *al-Tadhkira fī aḥwāl al-mawtā wa-umūr al-ākhira*, Cairo 1980.

Al-Qurṭubī, Muḥammad ibn Waḍḍāḥ, *Kitāb al-bida'*, ed. I. Fierro, Madrid 1988. (= al-Qurṭubī, *al-Bida'*)

Rasā'il al-'adl wa'l-tawḥīd, ed. Muḥammad 'Imāra, Cairo 1988.

Rasā'il ikhwān al-ṣafā', ed. Khayr al-Dīn al-Zirikly, Cairo 1928, repr. Beirut 1957.

Al-Rasā'il al-sab'a fi'l-'aqā'id, Ḥaydarābād 1948. (= *al-Rasā'il al-sab'a*)

Al-Rāzī, Muḥammad ibn 'Umar Fakhr al-Dīn, *Ma'ālim uṣūl al-dīn*, ed. Ṭaha 'Abd al-Ra'ūf Sa'd, Cairo n.d.

– *Mafātīḥ al-ghayb*, Dār Iḥyā' al-Turāth al-'Arabī, Beirut n.d. (= al-Rāzī, *Mafātīḥ al-ghayb*)

– *al-Maḥṣūl fī 'ilm uṣūl al-fiqh*, ed. Taha Jābir al-'Alawānī, Riyadh 1980. (= al-Rāzī, *al-Maḥṣūl*)

– *al-Nubuwwāt wa-mā yata'allaqu bi-hā*, ed. Aḥmad Ḥijāzī al-Saqā, Cairo and Beirut 1986. (= al-Rāzī, *al-Nubuwwāt*; part 8 of al-Rāzī's *al-Maṭālib al-'āliyya min al-'ilm al-ilāhī*, ed. al-Saqā, Beirut 1987. (= al-Rāzī, *al-Maṭālib al-āliyya*))

– *Sharḥ asmā' allāh al-ḥusnā-Lawāmi' al-bayyināt sharḥ asmā' allāh wa'l-ṣifāt*, ed. Ṭaha 'Abd al-Ra'ūf Sa'd, Beirut 1990. (= al-Rāzī, *Lawāmi' al-bayyināt*)

– *Muḥaṣṣal afkār al-mutaqaddimīn wa'l-muta'akhkhirīn min al-ḥukamā' wa'l-mutakallimīn*, ed. Ḥusayn Atay, Cairo 1991. (= al-Rāzī, *Muḥaṣṣal*)

Al-Shirāzī, Abū Isḥāq Ibrāhīm ibn 'Alī, *Kitāb al-ishāra ilā madhab ahl al-ḥaqq*, ed. M. Bernand, *La Profession de foi d'Abū Isḥāq al-Shirāzī*, Cairo 1987. (= al-Shirāzī, *K. al-ishāra*)

Al-Subkī, Abū Naṣr 'Abd al-Wahhāb ibn 'Alī, *Ṭabaqāt al-Shāfi'iyya al-kubrā*, ed. Maḥmūd and Muḥammad al-Ṭanāḥī and 'Abd al-Fattāḥ Muḥammad al-Ḥilū, Cairo 1964. (= al-Subkī, *Ṭabaqāt*)

Al-Suyūṭī, Jalāl al-Dīn 'Abd al-Raḥmān ibn Abī Bakr, *Ṣawn al-manṭiq wa'l-kalām 'an fannay al-manṭiq wa'l-kalām*, ed. 'Alī Sāmī al-Nashshār and Su'ād Alī 'Abd al-Rāziq, Alexandria 1970. (= al-Suyūṭī, *Ṣawn*)

– *Miftāḥ al-janna fi'l-i'tiṣām bi'l-sunna*, ed. Badr ibn 'Abd Allāh al-Badr, Beirut 1993. (= al-Suyūṭī, *Miftāḥ al-janna*)

Al-Ṭabarī, Abū Ja'far Muḥammad ibn Jarīr, *Jāmi' al-bayān fī tafsīr al-qur'ān*, Būlāq AH 1323 [AD 1905], repr. Beirut 1986. (= al-Ṭabarī, *Tafsīr*)

Al-Tabrīzī, Muḥammad ibn 'Abd Allāh, *Mishkāt al-maṣābīḥ*, ed. Muḥammad Nāṣir al-Dīn al-Albānī, Beirut 1961.

Al-Taymī, Abū al-Qāsim Ismā'īl ibn Muḥammad, *al-Ḥujja fī bayān al-maḥajja wa-sharḥ 'aqīdat ahl al-sunna*, ed. Muḥammad ibn Rabī', Riyadh 1990. (= al-Taymī, *al-Ḥujja*)

Al-Ṭūsī, Muḥammad ibn al-Ḥasan, *al-Iqtiṣād fīmā yat'allaqu bi'l-i'tiqād*, Beirut 1986. (= al-Ṭūsī, *al-Iqtiṣād*)
Yaḥyā ibn al-Ḥusayn, al-imām al-Hādī ilā al-Ḥaqq, *al-Radd 'alā ahl al-zaygh min al-mushabbihīn*, in *Rasā'il al-'adl wa'l-tawḥīd*, Cairo 1988, part 2, pp. 295–303.
Al-Zamakhsharī, Abū al-Qāsim Maḥmūd ibn 'Umar, *al-Kashshāf 'an ḥaqā'iq al-tanzīl wa-'uyūn al-aqāwīl fī wujūh al-ta'wīl*, Cairo 1972. (= al-Zamakhsharī, *al-Kashshāf*)
– *al-Minhāj fī uṣūl al-dīn*, ed. and tr. S. Schmidtke, *A Mu'tazilite Creed of Az-Zamakhsharī (d. 538/1144)*, Stuttgart 1997.
Al-Zarkashī, Muḥammad ibn Bahādir, *al-Baḥr al-muḥīt fī uṣūl al-fiqh*, ed. 'Abd al-Qādir 'Abd Allāh al-'Ānī, Kuwait 1992.

SECONDARY SOURCES

'Abd al-Raḥmān ibn Ṣāliḥ al-Maḥmūd, *Mawqif Ibn Taymiyya min al-Ashā'ira*, Riyadh 1995.
Abrahamov, B., 'Al-Qāsim ibn Ibrāhīm's Argument from Design', *Oriens* 29–30 (1986), pp. 259–84.
– 'Al-Qāsim ibn Ibrāhīm's Theory of the Imamate', *Arabica* 34 (1987), pp. 80–105.
– 'The Barāhima Enigma: A Search for a New Solution', *Die Welt des Orients* 18 (1987), pp. 72–91.
– 'A Re-examination of al-Ash'arī's Theory of Kasb according to Kitāb al-Luma'', *Journal of the Royal Asiatic Society* (1989), pp. 210–21. (= Abrahamov, 'A Re-examination')
– *Al-Qāsim ibn Ibrāhīm on the Proof of God's Existence Kitāb al-Dalīl al-Kabīr*, Islamic Philosophy and Theology Texts and Studies vol. 5, Leiden 1990. (= Abrahamov, *al-Qāsim*)
– 'Ibn Taymiyya on the Agreement of Reason with Tradition', *The Muslim World* 82:3–4 (1992), pp. 256–72. (= Abrahamov, 'Ibn Taymiyya')
– 'Abd al-Jabbār's Theory of Divine Assistance (*Luṭf*)', *Jerusalem Studies in Arabic and Islam* 16 (1993), pp. 41–58. (= Abrahamov, ''Abd al-Jabbār's Theory')
– 'Al-Ghazālī's Supreme Way to Know God', *Studia Islamica* 77 (1993), pp. 141–68. (= Abrahamov, 'Al-Ghazālī's Supreme Way')
– 'Necessary Knowledge in Islamic Theology', *British Journal of Middle Eastern Studies* 20 (1993), pp. 20–32. (= Abrahamov, 'Necessary Knowledge')
– 'The Appointed Time of Death (Ağal) according to 'Abd al-Ğabbār', *Israel Oriental Studies* 13 (1993), pp. 8–38.
– 'The *Bi-lā Kayfa* Doctrine and its Foundations in Islamic Theology', *Arabica* 42:3 (1995), pp. 365–79. (= Abrahamov, *Bi-lā Kayfa*)
– *Anthropomorphism and Interpretation of the Qur'ān in the Theology of al-Qāsim ibn Ibrāhīm – Kitāb al-Mustarshid*, Islamic Philosophy Theology and Science Texts and Studies, vol. 26, Leiden 1996. (= Abrahamov, *Anthropomorphism*)
Arberry, A. J., *Revelation and Reason in Islam*, London 1971. (= Arberry, *Revelation and Reason*)
– *The Koran Interpreted*, Oxford 1983.
Bello, I. E., *The Medieval Islamic Controversy between Philosophy and Orthodoxy:*

Ijmāʿ and Taʾwīl in the Conflict between Al-Ghazālī and Ibn Rushd, Islamic Philosophy and Theology Texts and Studies, vol. 3, Leiden 1989.

Bernand, M., 'L'Iǧmāʿ chez ʿAbd al-Ǧabbār et l'objection d'an-Naẓẓām', *Studia Islamica* 30 (1969), pp. 27–38.

– *L'Accord unanime de la communauté comme fondement des statuts légaux de l'islam d'après Abū al-Ḥusain al-Baṣrī*, Collection Études musulmanes XI, Paris 1970.

– 'Nouvelles remarques sur *l'iǧmāʿ* chez le Qāḍī ʿAbd al-Ǧabbār', *Arabica* 19 (1972), pp. 78–85.

Burton, J., *An Introduction to the Ḥadīth*, Edinburgh 1994. (= Burton, *Introduction*)

Calder, N., 'Ikhtilāf and Ijmāʿ in al-Shāfiʿī's Risāla', *Studia Islamica* 58 (1983), pp. 55–81. (= Calder, 'Ikhtilāf and Ijmāʿ')

Coulson, N. J., *A History of Islamic Law*, Edinburgh 1964.

Daiber, H., 'The Creed (*ʿAqīda*) of the Ḥanbalite Ibn Qudāma al-Maqdisī', *Studia Arabica et Islamica*, Festschrift Iḥsān ʿAbbās, ed. Wadād al-Qāḍī, Beirut 1981, pp. 105–25. (= Daiber, 'Ibn Qudāma')

– 'Abū Ḥātim al-Rāzī (10th century A.D.) on the Unity and Diversity of Religions', in *Dialogue and Syncretism: An Interdisciplinary Approach*, ed. J. Gort, H. Vroom, R. Fernhout and A. Wessels, Amsterdam 1989, pp. 87–104.

Davidson, H. A., *Proofs for Eternity, Creation and the Existence of God in Medieval Islamic and Jewish Philosophy*, Oxford 1987.

Dickinson, E. N., *The Development of Early Muslim Ḥadith Criticism: The 'Taqdima' of Ibn Abī Ḥātim al-Rāzī (d. 327/938)*, unpublished Ph.D. thesis, Yale University 1992, photocopied by UMI, Ann Arbor 1995. (= Dickinson)

The Encyclopaedia of Islam, Leiden 1960–. (= *EI2*)

Encyclopedia Iranica, ed. E. Yarshater, London, Boston and Henley 1985–.

The Encyclopedia of Religion, ed. M. Eliade, New York and London 1987.

Ess, J. van, 'Skepticism in Islamic Religious Thought', *al-Abḥāth* 21 (1968), pp. 1–18.

– 'The Logical Structure of Islamic Theology', in *Logic in Classical Islamic Culture*, ed. G. E. von Grunebaum, Wiesbaden 1970, pp. 21–50. (= van Ess, 'The Logical Structure')

– *Anfänge Muslimischer Theologie*, Beirut 1977. (= van Ess, *Anfänge*)

– 'Some Fragments of the *Muʿāraḍat al-qurʾān* Attributed to Ibn al-Muqaffaʿ', *Studia Arabica et Islamica*, Festschrift Iḥsān ʿAbbās, ed. Wadād al-Qāḍī, Beirut 1981, pp. 151–63.

Frank, R. M., 'The Neoplatonism of Ǧahm Ibn Ṣafwān', *Le Muséon* 78 (1965), pp. 395–424. (= Frank, 'The Neoplatonism')

– 'Several Fundamental Assumptions of the Basra School of the Muʿtazila', *Studia Islamica* 33 (1971), pp. 5–18.

– *Beings and their Attributes: The Teaching of the Basrian School of the Muʿtazila in the Classical Period*, Albany 1978.

– 'Reason and Revealed Law: A Sample of Parallels and Divergences in Kalām and Falsafa', *Recherches d'Islamologie – Recueil d'articles offert à George C. Anawati et Louis Gardet par leurs collègues et amis*, Louvain 1978, pp. 124–9.

– 'Al-Ghazālī on Taqlīd. Scholars, Theologians, and Philosophers', *Zeitschrift für Geschichte der Arabisch–Islamischen Wissenschaften* 7 (1991–2), pp. 207–52.

– *Al-Ghazālī and the Ash'arite School*, Durham and London 1994.
Friedmann, Y., 'Finality of Prophethood in Sunni Islam', *Jerusalem Studies in Arabic and Islam* 7 (1986), pp. 177–215.
Gimaret, D., 'Les Uṣūl al-Khamsa du Qāḍī 'Abd al-Ǧabbār et leurs commentaires, *Annales Islamologiques* 15 (1979), pp. 47–96.
– *Les noms divins en islam, exégèse lexicographique et théologique*, Paris 1988.
– 'Cet autre théologien Sunnite: Abū L-'Abbās Al-Qalānisī', *Journal Asiatique* 277:3–4 (1989), pp. 227–62.
– *La doctrine d'al-Ash'arī*, Paris 1990.
Goldziher, I., 'Catholic Tendencies and Particularism in Islam', tr. from 'Katholische Tendenz und Partikularismus im Islam', *Beiträge zur Religionswissenschaft* 1 (1913/14), pp. 115–42, in M. L. Swartz, *Studies in Islam*, pp. 123–39. (= Goldziher, 'Catholic Tendencies and Particularism')
– *Die Richtungen der Islamischen Koranauslegung*, repr. Leiden 1952; tr. into Arabic by 'Abd al-Ḥalīm al-Najjār, *Madhāhib al-tafsīr al-islāmī*, Cairo 1955.
– *Muslim Studies*, tr. from the German by C. R. Barber and S. M. Stern, ed. S. M. Stern, London 1971.
– *The Ẓāhiris, Their Doctrine and Their History*, tr. from the German and ed. by W. Behn, Leiden 1971. (= Goldziher, *The Ẓāhiris*)
Gutas, D., *Avicenna and the Aristotelian Tradition: Introduction to Reading Avicenna's Philosophical Works*, Islamic Philosophy and Theology Texts and Studies, vol. 4, Leiden 1988.
Hallaq, W. B., *Ibn Taymiyya against the Greek Logicians*, Oxford 1993.
Hourani, G. F., *Reason and Tradition in Islamic Ethics*, Cambridge 1985.
– 'Reason and Revelation in Ibn Ḥazm's Ethical Thought', in idem, *Reason and Tradition in Islamic Ethics.*
– 'The Basis of Authority of Consensus in Sunnite Islam', in idem, *Reason and Tradition in Islamic Ethics.*
Juynboll, G. H. A., *Muslim Tradition: Studies in Chronology, Provenance and Authorship of Early Ḥadīth*, Cambridge 1983.
Kraemer, J. L., *Humanism in the Renaissance of Islam*, Leiden 1986.
Laoust, H., *Essai sur les doctrines sociales et politiques de Taqī-D-Dīn Aḥmad b. Taimīya*, Cairo 1939. (= Laoust, *Essai*)
Lazarus-Yafeh, H., 'Some Notes on the Term *Taqlīd* in the Writings of al-Ghazzālī', *Israel Oriental Studies* 1 (1971), pp. 249–56.
– *Studies in al-Ghazzālī*, Jerusalem 1975.
Madelung, W., *Der Imam al-Qāsim ibn Ibrāhīm und die Glaubenslehre der Zaiditen*, Berlin 1965.
– 'The Spread of Māturīdism and the Turks', *Actas do IV Congresso de Estudos Árabes e Islâmicos, Coimbra-Lisboa 1968*, Leiden 1971, pp. 109–68.
– 'The Origins of the Controversy concerning the Creation of the Koran', *Orientalia Hispanica* 1 (1974), pp. 504–25.
– *Religious Schools and Sects in Medieval Islam*, London 1985.
– *Religious Trends in Early Islamic Iran*, Albany NY 1988. (= Madelung, *Religious Trends*)
– 'The Late Mu'tazila and Determinism: The Philosophers' Trap', *Yad Nama* in memoria di Alessandro Bausani, Rome 1991, pp. 245–57.
Makdisi, G., 'Hanbalite Islam', tr. (from French: 'L'Islam Hanbalisant', *Revue des Études Islamiques* 42 (1974), pp. 211–44; 43 (1975), pp. 45–76)

and ed. M. L. Swartz, *Studies in Islam*, Oxford 1981, pp. 216–64.
Melchert, C., 'The Adversaries of Aḥmad Ibn Ḥanbal', *Arabica* 44 (1997), pp. 234–53. (= Melchert, 'The Adversaries')
Pavlin, J., 'Sunni Kalam and Theological Controversies', in *History of Islamic Philosophy*, ed. S. H. Nasr and O. Leaman, London and New York 1996, vol. 1, ch. 7, pp. 105–18.
Pessagno, J. M., 'Intellect and Religious Assent', *The Muslim World* 69 (1979), pp. 18–27. (= Pessagno, 'Intellect')
Peters, J. R. T. M., *God's Created Speech: A Study in the Speculative Theology of the Mu'tazili Qāḍī l-Quḍāt Abū l-Ḥasan 'Abd al-Jabbār bn Aḥmad al-Hamadhānī*, Leiden 1976.
Plato, *Laws*, tr. B. Jowett, 3rd edn, Oxford 1892.
Powers, D. S., 'On the Abrogation of the Bequest Verses', *Arabica* 29 (1982), pp. 246–95.
Reinhart, A. K., *Before Revelation: The Boundaries of Muslim Moral Thought*, New York 1995. (= Reinhart, *Before Revelation*)
Rippin, A., 'Lexicographical Texts and the Qur'ān', in idem (ed.), *Approaches to the History of the Interpretation of the Qur'ān*, Oxford 1988, pp. 167–71.
Rubin, U., *The Eye of the Beholder: The Life of Muḥammad as Viewed by the Early Muslims*, Princeton 1995.
Schmidtke, S., *The Theology of al-'Allāma al-Ḥillī (d. 726/1325)*, Berlin 1991.
Schwarz, M., 'The Letter of al-Ḥasan al-Baṣrī', *Oriens* 20 (1972), pp. 15–30.
Sklare, D. E., 'Yūsuf al-Baṣīr: Theological Aspects of his Halakhic Works', in *The Jews of Medieval Islam: Community, Society and Identity*, ed. D. Frank, Leiden 1995, pp. 249–70.
Stroumsa, S., 'From Muslim Heresy to Jewish-Muslim Polemics: Ibn al-Rāwandī's *Kitāb al-Dāmigh*', *Journal of the American Oriental Society* 107:4 (1987), pp. 767–72.
– 'The Blinding Emerald: Ibn al-Rāwandī's *Kitāb al-Zumurrud*', *Journal of the American Oriental Society* 114:2 (1994), pp. 163–85.
Swartz, M. L. (tr. and ed.), *Studies in Islam*, Oxford 1981.
Tritton, A. S., 'Reason and Revelation', in *Arabic and Islamic Studies in Honor of Hamilton A. R. Gibb*, ed. G. Makdisi, Leiden 1965, pp. 619–30.
Wansbrough, J., *Quranic Studies: Sources and Methods of Scriptural Interpretation*, Oxford 1977. (= Wansbrough, *Quranic Studies*)
Watt, W. M., 'Early Discussions about the Qur'ān', *The Muslim World* 40 (1950), pp. 27–40, 96–105.
– *The Formative Period of Islamic Thought*, Edinburgh 1973. (= Watt, *The Formative Period*)
– (tr.), *Islamic Creeds: A Selection*, Edinburgh 1994.
Wensinck, A. J., *The Muslim Creed, Its Genesis and Historical Development*, repr. of the Cambridge edn (1932), London 1965. (= Wensinck, *The Muslim Creed*)
Wolfson, H. A., *The Philosophy of the Kalam*, Cambridge MA 1976. (= Wolfson, *Kalam*)

INDEX